Broken By You

Men's Role in Stopping Woman Abuse

Morton Paterson

THE UNITED CHURCH PUBLISHING HOUSE

Broken By You: Men's Role in Stopping Woman Abuse

Canadian Cataloguing in Publication Data

Paterson, Morton, 1935-
Broken by you

Includes bibliographical references and index.

ISBN 1-55134-033-X

1. Wife abuse - Religious aspects - Christianity. 2. Abusive men - Pastoral counseling of. 3. Abused women - Pastoral counseling of. 4. Church work with abused women. I. Title.

BV4445.5.P37 1995 261.8'35'872 C94-932571-6

The United Church Publishing House
3250 Bloor St. West
Etobicoke, Ontario, Canada
M8X 2Y4

Book Design: Dept. of Graphics and Print, First Image
Printed in Canada

Dedication

To friends on the Family Justice Committees of
East Plains United Church, Burlington
and
First United Church, Mississauga
who never gave up
when others said, "What's the Use?"

With affection,
and gratitude.

For I received from the Lord what I also handed on to you, that the Lord Jesus on the night when he was betrayed took a loaf of bread, and when he had given thanks, he broke it and said, "This is my body, that is [broken] for you. Do this in remembrance of me."

— I Corinthians 11:23b-24

This Is My Body

This is my body
an orchard of pomegranates
eyes like doves
lips like a crimson thread
breasts like two fawns
   that feed among the lilies
rounded thighs like jewels
hands dripping with myrrh
stately as a palm tree
comely as Jerusalem
This is my body, shared with you.

This is my body
bone of your bone
flesh of your flesh
sanctifying the marriage bed
bearing the fruit
breasts rounded with babies
stretch marks tracing
   the pangs of childbirth
wrinkles tracing
   the streams of tears
This is my body, wedded to you.

This is my body
sacrilege — sacrifice
punched, kicked, slapped, bruised
stalked and pillaged
split lip, broken bones,
   battered heart
eyes like shadows
   of a civil war
where love is strong as death
and passion fierce as the grave
This is my body, broken by you.

How will you remember me?

Contents

Acknowledgements

I acknowledge with gratitude the women who have unburdened heavy hearts by sharing with me stories of being hurt at home. An arm broken. A punch during pregnancy. A head being held under the bathtub tap with the water slowly rising — until promising to behave. These pained and painful accounts are representative of the scores of disclosures of abuse which I have heard in the past eight years.

Those who told these stories honoured me by inviting me to walk with them on the dark side of memory or a current journey of fear. Context but not substance has been altered to remove any possibility of identification even behind the fictitious names used throughout.

I also want to thank the men who have recounted their own abusive histories in conversations in office, home, or coffee shop. In private or in group settings many men have unburdened themselves about how they had abused women. Their candour has shown me that, given time in a setting of trust, men *can* talk about the mind-sets and feelings that lead to controlling, manipulative, and abusive behaviour. The evidence for my conviction that abusive men *can* change is *their* changed lives. Some of their accounts are given here, but the emphasis is on women's stories.

I maintain regular contact with a man who is serving a life prison sentence for domestic homicide and with a university chum from the fifties who has just completed a five-year sentence for wounding his wife: a knife slash put out her eye. If any man reading this book thinks that he is "only" denigrating, isolating, or slapping his wife, that the abuse will not escalate, and that the scenarios set out here are exaggerations, ponder this: the two men who killed and maimed also thought that way... before!

I also acknowledge the encouragement I have received from colleagues in ministry to persist at those times when I wavered in my intent to put into print something about the church's awful (deadly!) silence concerning domestic violence. Over countless cups of coffee we have discussed the church's unique opportunities and obligation to be partners in both the "stopping" and "mending" process.

Most women clergy already engage, to some degree, in family violence ministry both pastorally and from the pulpit: their mark is upon many of the ideas that are woven into this book. Many male clergy have told me of their need for clergy-focused resources to help them place higher priority on ministry with abused wives. Their training, experience, and personal mind-sets have left them bewildered (even inept) as to how to be pastorally effective when an abusive home situation in the congregation is reported or disclosed.

To be sure, excellent resources written by women are already available, and my first advice to anyone concerned about the church's response to home violence is to read some of these outstanding books. Hopefully mine will not be redundant. I am trying to broaden the resource-base, to "pipe-line" women's stories and interpretations of abuse in ways that will engage men. I hope this book helps.

I thank Cambridge University Press and Roderick Phillips for granting permission to quote excerpts from his book, *Untying the Knot.* Eva Lundgren of the University of Uppsala, Sweden, has kept me informed of her ground-breaking work on abuse within Christian families; I am grateful for her permission to quote parts of it. Amnesty International (Canada) has kindly given permission to quote from a speech by former Secretary General Pierre Sané.

Staff members and former residents of shelters and family counselling agencies have helped me enormously to understand the dynamics of marital violence, especially "stalking," a recently identified form of abuse which males almost never experience.

My first systematic study of how the church might better minister with victims and perpetrators of violence was made possible by a McGeachy Research Scholarship in 1984. It provided an opportunity to interview many people in both Canada and Norway; the results were published as *Toward A Justice That Heals.* This book builds on my initial explorations. I thank the McGeachy family for their visionary generosity in making available these scholarships, the intent of which is to encourage serious study that will "inspire and challenge the church towards creative and faithful mission."

I also acknowledge with gratitude the cooperation and advice of the special Family Justice friends to whom this book is dedicated; it's the least I could do!

Ruth Bradley-St-Cyr, Managing Editor of the United Church Publishing House and editor of this book, wrote the poem "This is My Body" specifically for *Broken By You.* It expresses succinctly and lyrically the heartbreak which I try to articulate in story form. She and Catherine Wilson, Director of Publishing at UCPH, gave hard-headed, solid advice at each stage of writing as well as warm encouragement when the writing got tough. Jean Ward and Don Gillies responded with alacrity when invited to write the forewords. Leslie-Elizabeth King assisted me in the considerable research which lay behind "Reality, with Hope: A Darkside Lectionary."

Peter Gordon White, of UCPH, made me aware of related developments in the medical profession by directing me to a published paper written by his physician son on "breaking silence" with women patients. I am grateful to Peter for this and for his unfailing support and his conviction that this book needed to be written.

Finally, I want to acknowledge the quiet influence of my former wife, Ruth, who tried in vain to break through to me in the closing years of our twenty-five year marriage. I remained insensitive to the depths of loneliness which an always-busy husband inflicted on her. I am only now beginning to understand. She recently heard me preach on a text from "The Song Of Songs." She said to me afterwards, "You've changed."

We are now more than half-way through the Ecumenical Decade of Churches in Solidarity with Women (1988-1998). I hope that this book will help to keep the goals of the Decade before the church.

Morton Paterson
Uxbridge, Ontario
1995

Foreword

by Jean Ward

Take a group of women, any group of women. Put them together long enough and they'll start telling stories. Safe stories at first; about jobs, children, lovers, and growing old. And this same group of women, given the right moment, will eventually tell you the hidden stories, hidden from their most intimate companions, sometimes even from themselves. These hidden stories, after you've heard a few, start to sound achingly familiar. A boyfriend, an uncle, a stranger, their father, their husband; someone hurt them in a way that does not heal.

Even if it happened years ago their memories are as fresh as the present moment.

"I never told any one, not even my mother."

"I saw him thirty years later and he smiled and hugged me as if it had never happened."

"I still have nightmares and wake up thinking that I'm six years old with no safe place to run to."

"I'm afraid every time my daughter leaves the house, and until she walks through the door I don't believe she will return unharmed."

"The first time he hit me I was six months pregnant, and as he swung his arm toward me he shouted that no baby was going to become more important than him."

Morton Paterson tells stories too but the ones he tells are women's stories. This will make many women angry and suspicious. As a Maritimer I discovered at an early age that it was one thing to tell a Maritime joke if you were from the Maritimes yourself but quite a different matter to hear it roll off the tongue of an Upper-Canadian. Somehow our ability to laugh at ourselves as Maritimers was only a strength if the telling was ours. Morton Paterson's book about male violence towards women will seem as impertinent and offensive to some as joke telling at another's expense. My own response when I heard this book was being written was, "Who does this man think he is?" So what convinced me that the book was worthwhile? What turned me from skeptic to supporter?

Well first of all, I do not doubt the truthfulness of the stories. They are not exaggerated. In my own work with the national office of the United Church of Canada these stories are everywhere, waiting in the faces of the women and men who stay behind after a workshop is long over. People wanting to tell their story, many for the first time, tales of pain, humiliation, fear, and regret. I never get used to them. They startle and humble me as much now as they did fifteen years ago. They are stories drawn out of reluctant bodies, told against all that is reasoned and controlled.

Second, as I read the book I began to see that Morton's storytelling, rather than diminishing the stories was actually giving them something I can only describe as "added voice." Please do not misunderstand me. The added voice was not because a man was telling the tale but rather because a man was telling the story as if he actually got it; as if the stories called out of him, out of his male skin, a real and difficult response. And this made all the difference for me.

Morton says he wrote these stories for himself, for the men who choose to read this book, and for the women who trusted him enough to tell their hidden tales. He writes too, I think, in order to attest to the crowd of witnesses who follow him — the women whose stories have yet to be told, and the men who raised hands to break bodies and minds. Morton has been seared by women's stories — touched by the fires of the telling — and will never be the same again. He is marked and he wants other men to be marked too.

So he tells the stories as simply and as true to the speaker as he can. He says that he feels compelled to share the emotional depth of that encounter so that other men can experience some of the terror, sadness, and remorse that was his originally as the hearer. Morton's hope is that the stories will elicit a response, a moment of personal recognition; "Yes I've done this, or thought this, or believed this, or allowed this in others."

I won't hold my breath however as the silence of most men still continues to puzzle and frustrate me. Why, in the face of overwhelming evidence pointing to the extent of male violence, are not all good men rising in protest? Why is it that when I speak at a workshop on the rise of violence and the church's responsibility the absence of men in attendance is a given?

It is not because men aren't concerned and afraid for their children and loved ones. Over the years conversations with fathers cradling their child or showing me a snapshot of a niece, daughter, or son have convinced me that many men care. And men too are the victims of male violence; both as children and adults. So why are men so silent? As a woman who looks in from the outside I have come to see that the answers are not easy or quick ones. But certainly within the circles I travel women's discussions about male responsibility and lack of sustained male proactive response are often countered by men's stories about the powerlessness they feel in the face of women's accusations. "What is a man supposed to do?" is a common refrain I hear from men I work with, men I meet in workshops, and men I call friends.

First, men need to respond because any response is preferable to silence. I don't understand silence, it baffles and confuses me. In the silence I am left to presume that most men, knowing the tales of women's horror, are unable even to stand in solidarity much less take action. In the silence it is left to women to weep and mourn. So what is it that I want from men? I want more than feelings of guilt and remorse. I want some kind of reciprocity, a coming back to me of the man's own story. Give me back, in exchange for my stories of pain and fear some of your own fear. Give me something of yourself other than your analysis and your well-honed stories of reverse discrimination. Give me something from your gut, something that knows what it is to be terrified with no assurance of protection. Tell me about the dreams that keep you awake at night, the fear that you are not a good father or lover, the awful truthfulness of your loneliness. Tell me you hear my story and will stand with me as you are able and I will try to do the same for you. For it is only when you speak of your true self, in a way that does not silence or belittle my story, that I can feel the presence of your spirit with mine.

Essentially, what women want of men is to be their emotional and spiritual equals. They want men who will not blanche at women's stories, but hang in for the unpleasant details — men who will push away the guilt long enough to stand with them and begin to change the world. Because, as we all know, changing the world is not for the faint hearted. Dreaming and imagining a new world requires the intellect and emotional vulnerability of men and women together on a common quest. It involves rigorous thinking, talking, and being, in other words it involves men and women who are whole and in touch with their bodies and souls.

For men this will be particularly difficult because at this juncture of our history, despite the rhetoric of the "new man," a man who truly decides to stand with women takes a leap of faith akin to taking a free-fall off the side of a cliff. After all, we are still in a system that terrorizes young boys into being men so there is not a lot of support for a man who decides to take the leap. It is in fact a very isolating experience if the men I know and trust are any example. They become isolated, cut off from their brothers, within a system created and controlled by men. And it is in this isolation that the terrors and fears of men are strengthened. I hope this book will help dispel some of this isolation and that it will be seen as one man's way of reaching out and bridging the isolation between men who are ready to challenge the suffocating hold of patriarchy — a hold that destroys men as well as women.

In the winter of 1982 I wrote this poem after trying to sneak out of the United Church manse in a small rural Manitoba community to attend a meeting of the Manitoba Conference Women's Committee on Domestic Violence. It was five in the morning and I wanted the rest of the household to get a few more hours sleep before their busy day began. I succeeded in getting as far as the door when my oldest daughter appeared.

My daughter only three
cautions as I rush out the door:
"Don't stop on the road, Mommy;
somebody will hurt you."

Are little girls born
with this fear of dark
unlit streets
and being caught alone?

Visions of the kingdom
crowd into my mind:
of a world without fear
and little girls
not old at three.

Some years have passed since that incident. Sarah is now a teenager who walks the streets at night in clear defiance of those who would harm her. With some chagrin I recognize the roles have been reversed. Now I am the one who is afraid for her. "Don't go out in the dark," I say to her and she reminds me that her father and I were the ones who raised her to be strong and secure. So what is my problem she wants to know? Well, I am a member of the baby-boomer generation who thought we had changed the world and all too quickly discovered that we were no more safe in our female bodies than our grandmothers had been. The past twenty-five years have been tough ones for between-gender relationships. The etiquette on dating and sexual relationships has changed so as to be almost unrecognizable and we now know in graphic detail what goes on behind closed doors. It is no surprise then that some of us, male and female alike, are a bit paranoid.

However, the young men and women who hang around my house would say this is a product of my generation and that they believe a new age is coming in gender relations. I hope they are right but I am jaded enough to mistrust most winds of change; they have a habit of just blowing through. True change will need the concerted energies of all generations and both genders. It will need the support of institutions, the nurture of many adults, and the courage of men and women who will leap off cliffs together. It will need fathers who are able to model a new and compassionate malehood and mothers who are strong and whole. And it will need youth and children who are willing to believe again, on behalf of the world, in the coming of a new order.

Life is about risk taking, about living, being, and finding ourselves in vulnerable, perilous places. Morton Paterson puts himself there. Whether you agree with his analysis or not, he has opened himself up to start the conversation. I hope you, as the reader, stick around to the conclusion and continue the talk and dreaming that puts you in uncomfortable places. It is frightening to be going out into the unknown but there are a growing number of us out there and soon our stories will be heard roaring in the winds of change.

Reverend Jean Ward is program consultant, Family Education and Justice, Division of Mission in Canada in The United Church of Canada. She also chairs the Commission on Family Ministries and Human Sexuality, National Council of The Churches of Christ (U.S.A.).

Foreword

by Don Gillies

It was with decidedly mixed emotions that I agreed to write this foreword to Morton Paterson's book on woman abuse. While I was intrigued and drawn by the fact that a man would even attempt such a volume I was also anxious and apprehensive about the volatility of the subject itself.

Abuse is an issue about which feelings tend to run very high. The available statistics on family violence and relational abuse are appalling and the role of patriarchal structures in creating, justifying and perpetuating such interpersonal violence is undeniable. The outrage and impatience of many women is understandable. The complicity of many religious institutions is shameful.

Like the author, I am male and cannot know what it is to be a woman. Indeed, though I have only limited awareness of it, I benefit from the very patriarchal system that is under attack here, so the likelihood of being able to offer a credible foreword is pretty slim.

Three additional things about me make me suspect as a voice for change. First, I have spent much of my career as a pastoral psychotherapist, practicing empathic, non-judgmental listening while working toward client insight and growth. In my work with couples, this has involved being open to both sides of every argument. Second, I am a committed civil libertarian — an advocate of individual rights and freedoms and therefore an opponent of excessive social control, even when it is in response to public demand. Third, I am a Christian, by which I mean one who believes and trusts in God's unconditional love and in the spiritual power of forgiveness and reconciliation — graces that are offered to all, to abused and abuser alike, as channels of God's love and as signs of hope in a troubled world.

For none of the above do I feel apologetic. They are, after all, core values in my life and work. Yet I can see that, taken altogether, they might well incline me to be "soft" on abuse — to understand when I ought to confront, to advocate when I ought to protect, to forgive when I ought to hold accountable.

I need to be reminded that, in any adequate understanding of God, justice is the twin of love. They are two sides of the same coin. To be sure, justice without love is punitive and harsh. But the obverse is equally true — love without justice is sentimental and self-serving.

What is called for is a balance between the two; a stance that is at once compassionate and challenging, pastoral and prophetic. In responding to relational injustice, we need to offer something more than empathy and consolation, worthy as these might be. We need to "consider it, take counsel, and speak out" (Judges 19:30).

What fosters change in my own attitudes and perceptions is the experience of deep sadness in the presence of human suffering. Seldom have I been motivated to change by guilt, or even by shame. But, when I find it possible to take in the reality of another's pain, then and then only am I motivated to change.

This is why I needed, and others also need, to hear and be horrified by the stories in this book. For it is only when we are repelled and saddened by such violence and abuse that we are able to respond in a meaningful way. Only then can we move beyond the assumption that violence is a basic if unpleasant characteristic of the male gender. Only then are we likely to change the way we live our lives.

I am sobered and challenged by Elie Weisel's blunt reminder that "what hurts the victim most is not the cruelty of the oppressor but the silence of the bystander."[1] It is out of an unwillingness to be such a "silent bystander" that this book has been written. It is in that same spirit that I offer these introductory reflections.

The place to begin is with an acknowledgement of the scope and seriousness of the issue. As study after study has confirmed, abusive behaviour is rampant in our society. The most often quoted statistic simply reminds us of the percentage of spousal abusers who are male (ninety-five percent or more!). More startling, however, is the revelation that violence has occurred at least once in "two-thirds of all marriages," that "twenty-five percent of wives are severely abused" during the course of their marriage and that abuse is also directed toward children, the elderly, and partners within gay and lesbian relationships.[2]

But statistics alone will not convince us of the seriousness of the issue. Sometimes they can have the opposite effect. They simply numb our sensibilities. What we really need to do is to hear the individual stories of fear and pain, the poignant cries of the victimized. Only then are we likely to grasp the full extent of the problem. Only then are we likely to be moved from indifference to empathy and from empathy to action.

As a slogan, "zero tolerance" has obvious appeal. But, for me, it is too abstract to be totally helpful. And it is riddled with ambiguity. For example, how is one to know, in advance and in every situation, what will be experienced as abusive behaviour? More potent, by far, is the assertion that "no means no." My own consciousness-raising about the horror of abuse was clinched by the reading of Elly Danica's slim but powerful volume entitled *Don't: A Woman's Word*.[3]

Real-life stories are at the heart of this study. Ordinary human stories about ordinary people like ourselves. Stories of terror and victimization. Stories of struggle and liberation. Familiar stories. The kind that I have heard many times, both as pastor and as therapist. Heartbreaking stories. Stories that need to be taken seriously. Someone's life may depend on it.

As a man, I find this whole topic difficult and disturbing even though I understand, in a theoretical way at least, the critique of patriarchy. I recognize that, to a large extent, it is still "a man's world" and I am sure that, at times, I take advantage of my position and power. But I am also committed to the creation of a different kind of world — a world in which power is shared equitably and gender is not the determining factor.

For that reason, I am troubled by certain aspects of the so-called "men's movement" with its seductive invitation to rediscover authentic male "energy" and thus give expression to the "warrior" within. It is not the intention that concerns me, for, in the responsible literature, the "warrior psyche"[4] is portrayed more as a curse than as a blessing. Rather, I am concerned about the potential spin-offs from this heady stuff. In the face of widespread abusive behaviour it is surely counterproductive, even wicked, to suggest that "a certain kind of forceful, penetrating, active energy is one of the foundations of masculine identity."[5]

More persuasive, I suggest, and more hopeful too, is the suggestion that such behaviour is socially conditioned and culturally reinforced. It's not that things *have* to be this way. Rather, it's that, for a variety of reasons, we *want* them this way!

This is not to suggest that the solution will be either simple or easy. The roots of interpersonal violence and abuse are deep and complex. Yet it is within our power, over time, to alter the style and content of our socialization. Indeed, there are encouraging signs that this may be happening already in some quarters.

There is much uncertainty in the air these days, especially in relation to established social institutions, like marriage, familiar gender roles, and other patterns of human interaction. Men have reason to be anxious and uncertain. But that must not become the rationale for a hostile backlash. Rather, it should be seen as an opportunity for personal transformation and for mutual growth.

Another reality, of course, is the complicity of religion in all of this. Too often, the Bible is misused in support of male superiority and female subordination, both in marriage and in other social structures. It is a point of view that has been underscored by theologians and proclaimed by churches in every age, including our own. Turning it around is not going to be easy. But turn it around we must, if we are to be faithful stewards of the truth we have been given.

At the same time, I am troubled by some current attitudes toward alleged perpetrators of violence and abuse. In the suggestion that suspected abusers should be considered "guilty until proven innocent," and in much of the hard-edged talk about vengeance, I detect a distressing swing of the pendulum. It would be neither helpful nor wise to bypass "due process" in order to deal with seemingly "obvious" perpetrators. "Two wrongs," as they say, "do not make a right!" Indeed, unless we move with deliberateness and care, the "last state" could turn out to be "worse than the first" (Matthew 12:45).

There is much in the news these days about the harm done and the pain caused by false and malicious charges of abuse. Such activities only fuel that ever-present and potentially destructive backlash. More helpful, by far, is the suggestion of Marie Fortune and others that great care must be taken in the definition and interpretation of abuse. To define it as "anything in a relationship which is unpleasant"[6] is to distort it beyond recognition and, even worse, to trivialize it beyond consideration. Broken relationships can be painful, but they do not always illustrate abuse. Such definitions, however well-intentioned, only detract from the real issue.

The same might be said of gender competition. Yes, there are cases of abuse where a man or boy rather than a female is the victim. But what is at stake here is too important to be sidetracked in this way. It is not a question of which wrong deserves our attention and our concern. Obviously, both do! It is not an issue of either/or but rather of both/and! We need to keep our eye on the goal. We need to work together to eradicate all forms of injustice. Above all, we need to remember that lives are at stake.

The path chosen in *Broken By You* is a rough one — indeed, it is a mine-field of potentially explosive misunderstandings. What business does a man have telling women's stories and drawing particular conclusions from them? By what authority does he pronounce our guilt or complicity as men and challenge us to become agents of transformation?

Yet that is where the author wants to take us. By sharing with disarming candour the story of his own awakening (conversion), he invites us to be open and vulnerable ourselves. By sharing these painful stories of abuse, he compels us to examine our own attitudes and actions. By exposing the complicity of religion in this social nightmare, he challenges people of faith to examine themselves, their theologies, and their institutions with the aim of achieving genuine repentance, reformation, and renewal.

Finally, by grounding his argument in the biblical witness, he reminds us of the brooding presence of One who not only suffers with the oppressed but also expects us to do something about their oppression. For that, especially, we are deeply in his debt.

Reverend Don Gillies is a United Church minister and an experienced pastoral psychotherapist. He is currently Director of Field Education at Emmanuel College in Toronto and is a teaching supervisor with the Canadian Association for Pastoral Practice and Education (CAPPE).

Preface

A book about life and death.

Your life. New life if you are a woman who has been belittled or broken in your own home, emptied of self-esteem, driven from the truth of who you are as God's cherished one.

Your death. A total emptying out of patriarchal mind-sets and attitudes if you are a husband who has hurt your wife mentally, physically, or sexually.

Your life. New birth if you are such a husband, but prepared to undergo such an emptying for your wife; to start fresh after naming your hurting ways. If you are willing to repudiate those parts of the old self that were capable of deliberate wounding.

Your life. If you are a man who has not hurt women, then you can deepen your awareness of the ways their bodies, hearts, and souls are broken behind the doors of home. By so doing you will become more alert as to how you may contribute to zero tolerance of abuse.

Their death. A memorial to those countless women who have been killed by their husbands, for whom the flame of the spirit was snuffed out in an evil moment of hot rage or cool deliberation.

Their life. A new chance for normalcy for children who have quivered in fear as parents scream at one another, as dad strikes and mum falls, in battle-zone homes where fear reigns.

In this book I invite you to enter into the power struggle that is waged against one of every four women at some time in her life, in which husbands maintain the centuries-old belief that they are the head and their wives are subordinate. And before you dismiss this problem as pertaining only to other houses on your street, I urge you to take the plunge into a radical inventory of the ways in which you and your partner converse, solve problems, and make decisions, the ways in which you critique one another, and the patterns of intimacy which fold you into one another's arms.

If you and your spouse believe that your marriage is a partnership rather than a power struggle, then you are blessed. You have the kind of relationship which you prayed for and expected on your wedding day. Be glad. Be grateful. For in your marriage you have preserved the mutual honouring and cherishing which your vows were all about. But remember, divorce and abuse statistics show that this is the exception and not the rule.

You may ask "How can a *man* write knowledgeably and helpfully about woman abuse?" This is a fair question, and has been asked often in the eight years that this book has been in the making. The only answer I can give is that I believe it is the responsibility of men, not women, to stop the abuse. Many years ago when Golda Mier was President of Israel a discussion arose in Parliament about how to protect women from violence by men. One proposal was to set a curfew for women so that they would be out of harm's way at night. Mier agreed that a curfew might be a good idea, but a curfew for men, not women, since men created the problem.

The topic then was violence outside the home but the issue is the same inside. Men must be held accountable for their behaviour; they, and not women, must be held accountable; they, and not women, must change their ways. As a man I have tried to change my own life-long patriarchal assumptions about who's in charge and, as a man, I address other men and urge them to so the same. I hope that, in this way, I may have something useful to offer to the stopping of woman abuse.

In most hurt-at-home stories that I've heard *husbands did not see themselves as abusive* so I am forced to conclude that the vast majority of men do not recognize in themselves either the control mind-sets which prepare the ground for manipulative abuse, or the degree to which some words or behaviour toward their wives are abusive. Deliberate or unintentional, the emotional or physical wounding of one's wife is common. *Whenever* the subject is raised among women, one hears such remarks as, "Someone I know has been hurt like that — but what can we do?"

Lots. Starting with a challenge to men!

IF you have ever hurt your wife;

IF you have ever manipulated or belittled her, pushed or struck her, or "persuaded" her into sex against her will;

IF you have hurt her but did not realize that you were;

IF you don't think you have a responsibility in helping end woman abuse;

THEN *listen* to the women you will meet in this book.

I'd like to borrow a statement made on Human Rights Day, 1993, by the Secretary General of Amnesty International, Pierre Sané, and apply it to the abrogation of human rights which is woman abuse:

> ...we can break the cycle of despair and carnage:
>
> No one, anywhere, can say, "I did not know."
>
> No one, anywhere, can say, "I did not know what my responsibilities were."
>
> No one, anywhere, can say, "I did not know what to do."

The first thing a man can do is take woman abuse seriously. If someone had asked me fifteen years ago whether I ever hurt my wife emotionally, physically, or sexually, I would have said, "Why, no! What a strange question for you to ask." If pressed further about whether any of my personal mind-sets might give rise to abuse, my reply would have been, "No way!" If the questioner persisted, "Have you, as a minister, ever dealt with woman abuse from the pulpit or in a discussion series?" my exasperated answer would likely have been, "No; there are too many other more pressing demands on my time. It isn't that big a problem in congregations, and besides I don't know anything about it."

In fact, the incidence of woman abuse is the same within church families as without; twenty-nine percent of women are being abused or have been abused by a present or former spouse (see Appendix III). Woman abuse does not start with the first put-down, the first back-hander across the mouth, or the first coerced sexual act. It starts with a long-held perception that men have a kind of divine right to control women. Men set the basic agendas in the worlds of politics, industry, civic affairs, sports, and religion so it should come as no surprise that the most basic and primordial arena of male control is the family. The unstated and unchallenged male belief in the *right* to dominance makes some form of woman abuse possible, even predictable.

A recent, comprehensive, and coast-to-coast project coordinated by The Canadian Panel on Violence Against Women, produced a final report entitled *Changing the Landscape: Ending Violence — Achieving Equality.* The report concluded that

> Despite a wealth of research in the area, we have only educated guesses of the prevalence of violence against women in Canada today. No matter what methodology is used, the figures are consistently alarming and ... underestimate the incidence of violence.[1]
>
> Consider these *underestimated* figures from the report:
>
> - 27 percent of women have experienced a physical assault in an intimate relationship.
> - In 25 percent of these cases, women who were physically assaulted reported that their partners explicitly threatened to kill them.
> - In 36 percent of the cases, women reporting physical assault also reported that they feared they would be killed by their male intimate ... the fury and violence exhibited during attacks made them fear for their lives.
> - 50 percent of the women reporting physical assault also experienced sexual assault in the context of the same relationship.
> - In 1991, 270 women in Canada were murdered; 121 were killed by intimate partners.[2]

If you still believe that the problem is not all that serious, then listen closely to the women you will meet in this book. Invite a staff member of your nearest women's shelter to speak to your group. Keep track of the frequency of news reports about violence against women by a boyfriend or partner, bearing in mind that very few are ever reported. Ask psychiatric, therapeutic, or pastoral counsellors about the origin and extent of home-centred female low self-esteem and the suicidal impulses that often accompany it.

By now some men may want to say, "Hold on! Why such a gender-specific account? Why not discuss spouse abuse?" My decision to deal only with woman abuse is *not* to make light of the approximately five percent of all spouse abuse victims who are male. But the statistics speak for themselves — ninety-five percent of spouse abuse victims are women — and the dynamics are different. Often, to some degree, self-defense is a factor. A separate treatment is clearly necessary.

The terms husband and wife are used throughout the book, but, for the most part, they are to be understood to include non-marital partner relationships as well. In *Changing the Landscape*, the expression "intimate relationship" is given a generic connotation. So too with my remarks about marriage violence. The imbalance and misuse of patriarchal power is the thread running through male/female marriage or non-marriage partner abuse.

A comment about biblical theology is necessary in order to clarify the spiritual setting of the book and explain the title. *Broken By You* derives from the words spoken by Jesus at the last supper, which have become the central phrase of the words of institution of the Sacrament of Holy Communion:

> The Lord Jesus on the night that he was betrayed took a loaf of bread, and when he had given thanks, he broke it and said, "This is my body that is [broken] for you. Do this in remembrance of me."
>
> — I CORINTHIANS 11:23b-24[3]

Shortly after Jesus' awesome action a squabble broke out about which of the disciples was greatest (Luke 22:24). What a sobering illustration of the spirit of hierarchical power-mongering which had infected the friendship circle which surrounded Jesus. We can only imagine the pain with which he responded:

> The kings of the Gentiles lord it over them; and those in authority over them are called benefactors. But not so with you; rather the greatest among you must become like the youngest, and the leader like one who serves. For who is greater, the one who is at table or the one who serves? Is it not the one at the table? But I am among you as one who serves.
>
> — LUKE 22:25-27

The sacramental breaking of bread is a "re-membrance" (a symbolic re-enactment, a "putting back together again") of Jesus' redemptive crucifixion. Mainline ecumenical Christianity (Catholic, Orthodox, Protestant) places central doctrinal emphasis upon God's saving act at Calvary. In various ways, and with a rainbow of degrees of sophistication, the church believes that Jesus' death was a complete "pardon" of the sin of all humankind. (Metaphors used to describe the meaning of the crucifixion have traditionally been judicial).

The "steadfast love" (in Hebrew, *chesedh*), or the "unconditional love" (in Greek, *agape*) of God were fully expressed by Jesus in the manner in which he lived, and in the self-emptying way in which he died. Such divine love is fundamentally a *healing* ("saving") force. Jesus entered into the pain of those he met. Particularly in the Gospel of Luke, (the "beloved physician"), he relates to people precisely at their point of greatest emotional, physical, and social need... as Dr. Jesus![4] In other words, religion — as understood and lived out by Jesus — is wrapped into the pain and healing of ordinary life.

But Jesus understood that his healing/saving work involved at its centre a deliberate self-emptying or relinquishing of power. He rebuked the disciples' Last Supper "I'm the greatest" obscenity. He refused to use control tactics in his relations with them.[5] He drew out from the hurting ones their *own* innate healing powers.

As his life moved inexorably toward crucifixion he presented himself as increasingly vulnerable — a weak one among weak ones. As he was being executed between two thieves he shrieked the abandonment words of Psalm 22:1: "My God, my God, why have you forsaken me?" This so-called cry of dereliction came from that place deep in the heart where all seemed lost. He *had* lost all. It was the final self-giving after a life of self-giving: "This is my body, broken for you."

Or *by* you... in the voice of woman crucified on the cross of male violence. The discipleship challenge to women is *not* to relinquish power or to cultivate vulnerability. Theologically, and in church life, women have traditionally been made powerless to begin with. Typically women have been encouraged by church and community to see themselves as essentially vulnerable. The gospel to women is *not*, then, an invitation to self-emptying servanthood. Rather it is the challenge to leave self-emptying behind, to reach out to and to grasp self-fulfilling equal power and an equal place at the Lord's table.

In her book, *Crucified Woman*, Doris Dyke reflects on the sculpture by the same name that was created by Almuth Lutkenhaus-Lackey and now stands in a garden at the University of

Toronto. This is one of several reactions to the sculpture Dyke quotes:

> The Crucified Woman does three things for me. Her form, the cruciform, haunts me as I see the image of Jesus, naked and tortured, and the image of the woman, naked and tortured, tumble over each other. She points me to Jesus, the Crucified One, the Lamb who was slain and now lives and reigns with God forever. But at the same time, she points me to all victims of violence who share in Jesus' communion of blood for our sins. She also of necessity points me to me. It is only the image and the heinous reality of the violent death of Jesus that has given me the tools I need to deal with the heinous reality of violence in my own life.[6]

Is the crucified woman your wife? Don't be quick to reply or deny. If she is, I say this to you: I have received from your wife what I hand on to you. At those times when you diminished, struck, or sexually coerced her she felt betrayed and broken in spirit. And while she gives thanks for what is good between you, she unfolds her arms before you and says, "This is my body, broken by you."

I believe that the church has a key role to play to help end woman abuse and provide a supportive healing environment in harmony with other caring individuals and agencies. The church, by its silence so far, must bear some responsibility for contributing to the problem and is morally bound to work with others toward solutions. The early Christian church was enflamed in spirit as it brought the message of Jesus' whole saving/healing peace to wounded and fractured women and men. In our day, I urge the church to relate that gospel to the specific world of hurting that happens behind the walls of home with the same fervour and urgency.

The three basic divisions of this book are Cry, Response, and Mending. For me the experiential realities of biblical salvation are the words "Help me," "I hear you," and "Your faith has healed you." In one way or another the perilous and unpredictable life journey can be scripted in terms of variations of these three phrases. One cries, hoping that someone will respond and that one will find mending and wholeness. This is the root idea of biblical "shalom-salvation." "Salvation" literally means "health" (from the Latin word *salus*). "Shalom" means "return to wholeness." Jesus' statement to the woman who touched his garment, "Daughter, your faith has made you well; go in peace" (Luke 8:48), is for me a slogan of hope, without which religion is barren.

The Cry, Response, Mending structure is therefore a pattern by which to discuss both the tragedy of woman abuse and some workable strategies of response and mending. By using this biblical model I hope to show that the overarching theme of salvation can be applied to the specific tragedy of woman abuse.

Men, if you see yourself in any of the chapters in Cry, then speak to someone you trust who can offer help and advice.

Women, if you hear an inner voice saying "That's me," and you've never tried to find a listener, don't wait another day. Your dignity, your self-esteem — maybe your life — depend on it.

Parents, if you suspect that your children have been damaged emotionally by seeing or hearing violence at home, then get help, for yourself and for them. Children assume that conflict is their fault and internalize that behaviour.

Adults, if you remember having been so damaged as a child, recognize that those noises and those sights have become part of the foundations of your adult years. If you saw violence at home then chances are high that you have experienced and/or inflicted some form of it yourself. Violence is cyclical. If you as a boy regularly saw Dad act superior and hit, your small mind was tucking away the "how males control" lesson for likely future application. If you as a girl regularly saw Mum diminished and hurt, you were being set up for the belief that being female involves being "put in her place."[7]

The stories recounted here involve women, men, and children with whom I have had direct contact. This is not a book to be "enjoyed" but if it helps anyone to anticipate a future without violence at home, then my purpose will have been fulfilled. If you, as a husband, are inflicting mental, physical, or sexual abuse, *please stop*. If you, as a wife, have been living in marital fear, say, "*No more, ever*!"

May the shalom-peace of God bring to wholeness those parts of your life that are scattered. You deserve that peace. Your faith, and your own hard work, will make you well... again.

PART I

CRY

My eyes cause me grief at the fate
of all the young women in my city.

— LAMENTATIONS 3:51

Chapter 1

The Divine Right of Husbands

> To the woman [God] said, "I will greatly increase your pangs in childbearing; in pain you shall bring forth children, yet your desire shall be for your husband, and he shall rule over you."
>
> — GENESIS 3:16

Men, wake up!

Women, keep ringing the alarm bells about the reality and the extent of woman abuse. It is taking men a long time to hear those bells, since, frankly, it's not in our best interests. A systematic male deafness blocks any admission that in every fourth home in Canada there lives a woman who has been or is being hurt physically, sexually, and/or mentally by her husband.[1] The entrenched myth of a man's *right* to rule in his own home is protected on all sides by men who have no desire to lose it.

The accounts of abuse that are presented here are augmented by reference to books, articles, songs, and videos which address woman abuse from a number of points of view. No one approach tells the whole story. What is sadly obvious is that there have been few attempts to understand the male refusal to hear the story. Yes, there are books, only a few written by men, that clarify the patriarchal underpinnings of male violence. They focus on the widespread tolerance of males hurting females and offer substitute models of what it is to be "a real man." Recent phenomena like men's support groups — the men's movement — "The White Ribbon Campaign," and "Men Walking Against Male Violence" draw increasing support from men and credibility from women. They give men a chance to declare in a public way a personal commitment to ending violence against women.[2]

It is only in recent years that my own anger buttons concerning violence against women have been pushed. It was a shock for me to discover that I too had bought into the male "right to rule" scenario. Until about twelve years ago I was among those males who do not want to recognize their assumption of a *biblically*-based husband-authority model.

It is a model which has played a major causal role in the ages-long development of patriarchy within the home. For the belief that a husband/father has an implicit and God-given *right* to control his wife and children is laced into both Old and New Testament theology of the family. Even though this right does not include explicit permission to hurt, it is the broad base from which abusive behaviour springs. From control to misused control is a short hop. It is an even shorter one from misused control to abuse.

Biblical support of the myth

It is important to realize that much of the male attitude around being head of the house is derived from centuries old and scripture-sanctioned notions of patriarchy. One could make only a soft connection between the myth of male dominance and Biblical family theology. One could say that the belief in a husband's right to dominate his wife just happens to be confirmed in some parts of scripture but not in others. In other words the connection is circumstantial, not systemic — certainly not a problem. Such a view takes the Bible "off the hook." Those who regard the Bible as a guide for the life journey have unfortunately often disregarded its theology of the family — a theology that sanctions a husband's position of superiority at home.

Before we look at some specific expressions of such a theology of the family, it is important to realize that the Hebrew word for Lord, *adon,* is one of the words for husband. The most fundamental meaning of that word — *adonai* — is "my master." When Moses asked God for a name, God's response (in the Hebrew text) was "*'ehyeh 'asher 'ehyeh*" or "Yahweh asher yahweh." It means "I am who I am," or "I shall be who I shall be" (Exodus 3:14). The written form of the name has remained Yahweh (or Jehovah), but the spoken form is *adonai*, my master. In order to avoid putting a holy mystery on one's lips it was agreed that God would be called Adonai — my Master or my Lord.

The plot thickens when you consider that another common word for husband was *ba'al.* It was derived from a verb which, in the widest sense, means "to own or possess, especially a wife."[3] Its basic meaning was also Lord or Master and it was eventually used in a derogatory sense to designate the gods of foreign nations. The *baalim*, or baals, were false gods; only Adonai was the true God.

The connection between Lord, master, and husband is most dramatically illustrated in the Book of Hosea. The prophet allegorically portrays the fallen and decadent Israel as Gomer, his bride who had fallen into unabashed whoredom. In these passages the word for wife is *'eshah*, which means simply "woman." Even though a third word — *'ish* — (man), is used here to mean husband, Hosea clearly has in mind the tie between Lord, Master, and husband when he rhapsodically expresses the *intent* of the covenant as a marriage relation between God and Israel:

> On that day, says the Lord, you will call me, "My husband," and no longer will you call me "My Ba'al." For I will remove the names of the Ba'als from her mouth, and they shall be mentioned by name no more. I will make for you a covenant on that day with the wild animals, the birds of the air, and the creeping things of the ground; and I will abolish the bow, the sword, and war from the land; and I will make you lie down in safety. And I will take you for my wife forever; I will take you for my wife in righteousness and in justice, in steadfast love, and in mercy. I will take you for my wife in faithfulness; and you shall know the Lord. (2:16-20)

God is husband; Israel is wife. The entire initiative for determining the terms of the covenant, noble as they are, is one-sided. Male acts/decides; female reacts/acquiesces. Hosea's allegory is a clear confirmation of a family power dynamic which had become the norm.

The allegory is repeated in the New Testament. The Church is the "Bride of the Lamb" (Christ) in Revelation 21:2,9. The initiating Divine figure is again male. The responding figure is female. I believe that any attempt to wash out these clear "male is superior" underpinnings of a family ethic as incidental is a serious mistake. In terms of the overall biblical freight of the words "husband" and "wife," the allegories simply would not "work" if the genders were reversed. It is inconceivable that Israel might have been described as God's dissolute husband or the Church as Christ's bridegroom. They work because the dominant marriage role applied to God or Christ is that of husband. Furthermore, woman has no voice in the biblical marriage covenant. The terms of the covenant consist of God's promise of righteousness, justice, steadfast love, and mercy. All that is expected of woman/wife Israel is obedience. She is to change her ways, to behave, and to be deserving of the Lord's largesse. Though the covenant is unconditional from the Lord's side, Hosea's prophesy sets out a graphic litany of misfortune that will befall the persistently unfaithful tribes of Israel.[4]

Shattered and Broken is one of the recent books on the church's role in family violence ministry. The authors, S. Rutherford Madill and Linda Madill, begin with a good overview of church-centered male abusive behaviour. Then they move to an astonishing defence of the "husband-as-head" model — a view that is tempered only by the husband's responsibility for using his God-given right in a non-abusive way:

> Man is ordained by God to play out his headship and authority by taking care of and nurturing those who are his responsibility... Paul described Christ's position as head of the church: "We will in all things grow up into him who is the Head, that is Christ." That is the picture of family relationship: the head leads the way for the whole body as it grows and builds up in love, as each member does his and her work.[5]

The Madills speak out of a conservative tradition in which beliefs that are enshrined in scripture have an implicit contemporary authority. Their idea of male headship is built on these texts from Paul:

> Christ is the head of every man, and the husband is the head of his wife, and God is the head of Christ.
>
> — I Corinthians 11:3

> Wives, be subject to your husbands as you are to the Lord. For the husband is the head of the wife just as Christ is the head of the church, the body of which he is the Savior. Just as the church is subject to Christ, so also wives ought to be, in everything, to their husbands.
>
> — EPHESIANS 5:22-24

Paul's view of marriage is *wrong*! We have to break free of a slavish assumption that the cultural traditions out of which scriptural texts arise have authority equal to the faith insights they convey. The main difference between such literalism and a contextual view of the Bible is that the latter attempts to disentangle the culture and faith strands, and to take into account the temporary nature of some moral views in the Bible.

A male headship model of marriage was current in Paul's time, but it is *not* in ours. There is no more reason to protect such a "husband-as-head" belief than there is to abide by the impurity codes of the book of Leviticus. This does not mean that we scrap culturally outdated passages. It would be philistine to wipe out references to the social and personal background of the spiritual truths in scripture. Even the "dark-side" biblical stories that demean women should be retained and not expunged. They need to be explored and challenged, not ignored.[6]

It is important to have some idea of the theological and biblical slant of any clergy you meet with to discuss an abusive situation. For if he or she is committed to a tradition that elevates *all* biblical texts to a pedestal of spiritual authority, then some assumptions around male authority and husbandly headship will likely be operating. You may be steered onto a track which leads to "nonabusive male superiority." This is a contradiction in terms; a male superiority view is inherently abusive. The goal of a self-help group or pastoral counselling is the full restoration of female dignity. That simply cannot happen if homage to a male headship model is not jettisoned first. Biblically-based and church-supported patriarchy is alive and well in many denominations and congregations across the land. It is the decayed earth in which woman abuse flourishes.[7]

Clergy, however, are not the only "authority figures" who have been unhelpful in paving the road from patriarchy to a more equitable society. The Canadian justice system in particular has been roundly criticized for its deadly tolerance of "domestic" violence. The laissez-faire attitude of some judges toward woman abuse is scandalous. An editorial in *The Globe and Mail*, published on December 13, 1993, noted several instances of outright misogyny:

- In 1987, the Nova Scotia cabinet fired a provincial judge who commonly advised women to "follow the Bible's teachings" and be subservient to their husbands, even if they abused them.
- In 1989, a Manitoba judge apologized after saying, "Sometimes a slap in the face is all that she needs," during a domestic assault case.
- In 1990, during an assault and weapons trial in a Montreal suburb, a senior judge said that "rules are like women: they are meant to be violated."
- In November 1993, Judge René Crochetière of the Quebec Court released a man accused of threatening to kill his wife. When the wife complained she might be killed as a result, Judge Crochetière replied: "If the gentleman assassinates the lady I won't lose any sleep over it and I won't die. Don't worry I won't suffer from a depression either, because it is not my responsibility."

The only saving feature of such candour is that those who hold such attitudes can be identified, challenged, and, hopefully, dismissed. Clergy always have the Bible — the word of God itself — to hide behind. One wonders how many esteemed male figures in community life also hold such views but mask them behind a "proper" public persona and "politically correct language." Parliament itself was embarrased just a few years ago when a gaggle of male MPs began laughing and jeering during a discussion of woman abuse.

But what of the average husband? Doesn't patriarchy have its benevolent side as well? Following are three brief stories which seem, on the surface, to be quite innocent. "I thought you'd agree" illustrates how a relatively low-level patriarchal dynamic is brought into a pre-marital relationship. There are many variations of this story; what husband has not made a significant family-life or financial decision without conferring with his wife first? Consider the potential evolution of this dynamic, however, if it had not been nipped in the bud.

I thought you'd agree

Samantha and Bill came hand-in-hand to see me for the first of four pre-wedding interviews. Even though I encourage couples to attend an ecumenical weekend marriage seminar, I still ask them to meet with me; the wedding is more personal that way. Besides some issues, like patriarchy, that would not likely surface in a large group can be identified and dealt with privately.

Part-way through the first interview, I asked Bill and Samantha about their work. Samantha was a cost accountant, and Bill a firefighter. As we were concluding our preliminary "getting-to-know-you" conversation, I asked if they had any questions. Bill said, "Well, umm, yes, I do have a question. Our fire station has a 1930's fire truck in mint condition. Do you have a problem with our leaving the church after the wedding in the fire truck. I've booked it."

Samantha jumped forward in her chair before I could give my answer. She exclaimed, "You've what?"

"Booked the fire truck. I wanted to surprise you, but figured I'd better check it out with the Rev. You'll love it."

"Bill, we're not leaving the church in a fire truck, vintage or not. I want us to leave the church in the same way as the rest of the wedding, not flashy or showy, just simple."

Bill was embarrassed. After a split-second look of annoyed surprise (during which he was undoubtedly saying to himself, "I knew I shouldn't have told her."), he said, "But I thought you'd like the idea."

"I don't, and I won't."

This was no time or place to settle what was obviously a potentially hot item. So I said, "Before our next appointment, please decide." They left — not holding hands.

A month later they returned, hand-in-hand. "Well?" I smiled. A light approach seemed best.

"We're not going to leave the church in a fire truck," Bill smiled back. "Maybe my attendants and I will arrive at the church with the siren cranked up. We've had a good talk. I was wrong to make that decision without talking it over with Samantha." Turning to her, he continued, "I'm really sorry; it seemed like such a small thing, a neat surprise."

Samantha added, "It's not that I'm a stick-in-the-mud. I do like surprises. I hope you'll treat me sometimes with things I'm not expecting. It's just that, for my wedding, you know, I want it to be quiet and a little elegant. Thanks for understanding."

The remaining discussions were delightful, as we explored at some depth several trust and communications issues. The wedding was joyful. No, the male wedding party did not come to the church on the fire truck. Not because Samantha was against the idea (she wasn't), but because Bill reconsidered, and thought that simple was better.

Not all brides-to-be would have leapt forward in their chairs. Many would have thought to themselves, "Oh no, I don't like the idea *at all*, but Bill is obviously so excited about it. I'll keep my mouth shut."

The issue was not the vintage fire truck. It was the male presumption that a decision affecting both could justifiably be made only by him. Lest one regard Samantha's recalcitrance as minimally significant for the way the relationship was to unfold, think about those marriages you know of where unilateral decision-making (by either party) is problematic.

This next pastoral incident also has a happy ending. A seemingly jocular yet nonetheless patriarchal marriage pattern which had developed over a fifteen year period was identified — hardly "in the bud" — but certainly in time to retrieve a woman's slipping self-image.

This one

Clark and Edna are middle-aged, friendly, and always fun to be with. Both their faces beam whenever you meet them. They seem happy; certainly Edna does not appear to be hurting in the marriage.

During a church Bible study session Clark had occasion to refer to Edna as "this one." I caught my breath, looked at him, and asked him if I'd heard correctly. "You called Edna 'this one'? Do you call her that often?"

"All the time," he grinned, "but she doesn't mind. It's just my way of being affectionate with... with 'this one'."

I turned to Edna. "Edna, how do you feel about being called 'this one'?" She smiled at first. Then her face clouded over. The Bible study group was obviously a comfort zone for her. She turned to Clark and said quietly, "Clark, I don't like being called that, but I never wanted to tell you."[8]

To the best of my knowledge, he's called his wife Edna ever since. A small concession to a touchy wife? Or a big lesson for a big man? I have kept in touch with them over a ten-year period. Clark's grin is broader than ever. Edna's eyes twinkle like flawless diamonds.

What's in a name? Enough to save or end a marriage. The following is only part of a story — but an important part.

She knows who I mean

Marvin never called his wife, Carol, by either her given name or a nickname when talking to her or about her. It wasn't all that obvious when I first met them, since it is not unusual for friends or partners not to use names explicitly in conversation. But after being with them socially a few times, it had become obvious, since Carol did call him by name.

Finally, when we were together with a very small group of friends, I asked, "Marv, you don't call Carol by name; how come?"

He replied, "She knows who I mean."

Carol said, "I'd love it if you'd call me by my name; you haven't for years. Please call me Carol again."

"Why?" he retorted.

For more complicated reasons than this, their marriage folded two years later. But the "first name" issue was surely a public indicator of private pain. How partners use one another's names or nicknames can be symptomatic of underlying uneasiness, or worse. Tone of voice, eye contact — even volume — can be the visible expression of a tender or a resentful heart. The first word attributed to Jesus after the resurrection in John's gospel is a name — "Mary" [20:16]. I picture it being said quietly, affectionately. No, I have no evidence of the *way* Jesus said Mary's name; it is an assumption based on the kinds of things I believe about him.

A woman who read the first draft of this chapter identified an unfair streak in my account of patriarchy. Initially I prickled at the criticism, but heard her out. Her comment was "You make it appear that men are twits; they aren't, you know. Bill, Clark, and Marvin are basically decent guys — thoughtless maybe, but decent. They don't deliberately hurt their wives, but seem unaware of being mildly irritating. And, except for Marvin, they *did* change."

My friend's critique played on my mind for some time. In our day "male bashing" has often taken on cruel and certainly unfair proportions. Was my discussion of patriarchal mind-sets on the cheap end of the fairness scale?

Admittedly, the behaviour I have described would not generally be regarded as abuse. Bill, Clark, and Marvin *are* fine men. And male-bashing for its own sake is both pointless and sexist. What I am trying to identify is "embryonic" abuse, long before it would be commonly identified.

In the mid-seventies I was part of a three-member university committee whose task it was to make a proposal aimed at setting up a Women's Studies programme. A female sociologist and I arrived early for a committee meeting, and were engaged in animated conversation before the third member, a male, arrived. After the meeting had ended, my sociologist friend invited me to her office. She was plainly agitated.

"What's wrong?" I ventured.

"Mort," she said, "you aren't going to like what I'm about to tell you. When a male came into the room you moved your chair to face him, making it necessary to look over your shoulder at me. Most of your remarks were directed to him, and on those few occasions when you spoke directly to me, or when I spoke, you kept looking at him. It was as if I wasn't there."

I was floored, and pleaded for a detailed account of both my "body language" and of her feelings during the meeting. As she put it later, she felt I could "take" a painful lesson in sexual politics. The bad news was my incredible ignorance about how shabbily I was treating a female colleague. The good news was her determination to call me on it. That conversation was a major stimulus toward the writing of this book.

Since then I have called many men on just these kinds of minor slights in language or behaviour, and my experience has been that the vast majority respond with a desire to know more about interactive patterns between men and women. My sociologist friend called me at just the right moment, and increasingly I believe that to do so is a way of honouring, not merely a form of criticism. To identify the possibly abusive direction of a frame of mind is meant to heal, not to hurt.

Men must remember that they stand to gain as much as women from the process of dismantling patriarchy. It is not true that only women will discover expanded self-awareness and stronger self-esteem through being honoured by their partners. Men too will have bigger hearts, will think better of themselves, and will grow in spirit through a mutuality model. The "I'm in charge" mind-set cripples whoever holds it as well as those who suffer from its application.[9] Changing these mind-sets benefits men and women equally in establishing loving partnerships.

The patriarchal mind-set does not necessarily *cause* woman abuse but it is the inevitable common factor. Any move toward a zero tolerance of woman abuse, therefore, must start with a zero tolerance of patriarchy, no matter how "innocent" a form it might take. I urge both women and men to *name* it and *challenge* it as soon as it raises its ugly head. Let there be no doubt in anyone's mind that, for you personally, the mere hint of a male feeling of superiority or even the cute "second-placing" of one's wife do not wash. You might be regarded as a humourless crank. But the "cranks" who don't laugh at racist jokes play a quiet but mighty role in the hoped for zero tolerance of racism.

So I say to Bill, Clark, Marvin, and to all men: you are invited on a journey of discovery. The road is not well travelled and is full of bumps and potholes, but the destination — a more loving and equitable relationship of two strong partners — makes the trip truly worthwhile.

Chapter 2

BEHIND EVERY FOURTH DOOR

It is not enemies who taunt me —
    I could bear that;
it is not adversaries who deal insolently with me —
    I could hide from them.
But it is you, my equal,
    my companion, my familiar friend,
with whom I kept pleasant company. . .

— Psalm 55:12-14a

A study done in November 1993 (see Appendix III) indicates that twenty-nine percent of Canadian women have been or are being abused by their male partners. This figure includes deliberate emotional or psychological abuse — what I shall call mental torture — as well as physical violence and threats of violence. The current estimate of the number of women who are or have been physically battered is one in ten. Half the women in this group speak of sexual abuse in the same relationship.

At least he didn't scold me tonight

It was to be a friendly evening of duplicate bridge in a couples' group. I had been invited to sit in for a husband who was out of town on business, so that his wife wouldn't have to miss the chance to play with the regulars. My bridge playing is mediocre, more "seat of the pants" than systematic, and I had never played duplicate before. I knew only a few people, and was edgy when the first hand was dealt.

The first dart was hurled during the opening hand. Jim's scowl at Betty was dark, even menacing. She had made what he thought was an outrageous response to his demand two bid. It didn't matter that he couldn't see her weak hand; after the round was played out it was obvious that her response had been the correct one, and that his continuing to a game bid was an angry risk based on the cards he thought Betty *should* have held. Of course he went down in flames, which led to a muttered growl and an even darker glare at his wife. Whatever Betty bid or played for the rest of that set brought on the same ugly response from Jim. It was a relief to move on to the next table.

If you think this is a pretty tame opening illustration of mental torture, then listen to the end of the story. As we chatted over refreshments after the tables had been folded and put away, I overheard Betty say nervously to a woman sitting next to her, "At least he didn't scold me tonight." I shuddered inwardly. If he was like this in public, what must he be like at home?

Is "torture" too strong a word to describe Jim's behaviour? I think not. Clearly his menacing glares — usually accompanied with rebuke and at least one kick under the table — were commonplace in their marriage pattern. It is too facile to say, "Well, why did she put up with it; I wouldn't have!" There are so many reasons why women stay in an abusive relationship. I tell this story frequently to illustrate mental torture in marriage. The first reaction (from women as well as men) is typically to lay blame on Betty for allowing the abuse to go on. I say "first reaction" because it reflects our deepest assumptions that abuse happens to "other people" and squares with the common "blame the victim" reaction which has been characteristic of our response to violence against women.[1]

This deep-seated tendency cannot be taken lightly, for it diverts serious attention away from the real issue. The issue is power. The abuse is Jim's *control* of Betty. However many years it took in their marriage for "honouring" to disappear, by now Betty has been totally manipulated into submission and acquiescence. If he glares at her at the bridge table how do you suppose he reacts to her driving, her hobbies, her meals — indeed, her friends?[2]

Mental abuse doesn't start on the wedding day or years into the marriage. It usually starts during the dating period with apparently small intimidations, direct threats, cajolings, and put-downs. If such initial controlling behaviors are unchecked, then over time they can become full-blown abuse.

There is some evidence for the suggestion that some women are "open" to abusive male behaviour, and in fact have grown up to expect it. If one was raised in a family in which it was part of daily life, then, absurd as it may sound, even violent behaviour patterns are internalized, and are regarded as "part of the package" of ordinary domestic life. This does not mean that an individual so raised "looks for" abuse, but rather that when it occurs it is not surprising. Too often a woman's first reaction to abuse is to believe that she provoked it; it was "her fault."

Many years ago I was made aware of a form of mental torture so cruel and indecent that I wondered how its victim was able to keep her sanity.

Hi honey, meet my girlfriend

Pamela, Murray, and their teenaged daughter, Julie, lived in eastern Ontario. In her early thirties Pam was thrown from a horse and rendered paraplegic. She coped quite well in a wheelchair at first, but eventually other nerve damage caught up with her and her bodily movement deteriorated even further. Murray was always seen as a model caregiver. When others were around he bent over backwards to meet her every need. He spoke to her lovingly, and occasionally touched her arm or shoulder with affection. Julie has always related warmly to Pam, never complaining when asked to help with a household chore.

During the five year period in which Pam's movements were getting more and more awkward, she frequently expressed gratitude to her church and community friends for their visits and the constant flow of bright greeting cards. They marvelled at her good spirit, reminding her that she was blessed to be married to a guy like Murray. Then there was a sea change.

Pam's friend Alice phoned me one day and asked if I would meet with Pam and herself at her home. Over coffee she disclosed a painful story of loneliness, deceit, and now cruel marital betrayal. For years Murray's behaviour behind the walls of home had been in stark contrast to what visitors saw. Since her accident he had been severe, verbally abusive, and sharply critical of her "holy

Josephine" church friends. If she needed a hand to maneuver her chair, he jolted it roughly. For about two years he had been making frequent and disparaging remarks about her lack of sexual attractiveness with comments like, "You sure aren't the chick I married." He had insisted that they sleep separately; Pam got the guest room.

As far as Pam could tell, Murray's abusive language and behaviour happened when Julie wasn't around. But, she told Alice, she thought Julie could surely "feel in the air" Murray's contemptuous attitude towards her mother.

Then the crunch came. The week before Murray had brought home a girlfriend. They walked past Pam on their way upstairs to the bedroom where Pam and Murray used to sleep together. A heart-broken Pam called Alice the next morning after Murray had gone to work and asked between sobs if they could get together. And even though Alice knew the scene well enough to recognize Murray's sham front, she could not believe her ears when told of the latest abuse.

Pam had no resources with which to leave the home, and a demand that Murray leave fell on deaf ears. Besides, despite the shameful turn of events, which were frequently repeated, she still loved him. Later, in a postcard from Greece where he had gone for a vacation with his girlfriend, Murray wrote, "I still love you." A twist of the knife.

After continuing to live in the same house for several months, Pam finally announced that she'd had enough. She started divorce proceedings.

You made the wrong choice

It was early in their marriage. George and Margaret came from quite conservative denominational backgrounds. Margaret knew that George's decision to enter theological college would mean three years of cracking the books and not a great deal of social life. The college that George entered on a scholarship had a more liberal ambiance than what they had been accustomed to, but they were convinced that they could hold on to values that might not be honoured to the same degree they did.

The first faculty-student social provided an opportunity to test that conviction. They had both been raised as teetotalers, and had not previously moved in circles where alcoholic beverages were available. They had not been at the social long before Margaret drew George's attention to the drinks table: there were two punch bowls, one labelled "with," the other "without."

Margaret was inclined to try the "with" bowl, just to see what it tasted like. She mentioned to George that she was toying with the idea. He responded coolly that it was her choice. She took a small glass, having learned that the fruit punch in the "with" bowl had been laced with vodka. She enjoyed the extra snap, but reverted to the "without" bowl for the duration of the social.

George did not speak to her for the rest of the evening, and suggested that they leave early; he'd had enough, and was obviously in a dark mood. In the car Margaret asked, "What's wrong?" His answer caught her off guard, and to this day she believes that it set the tone for her life-long deferential attitude toward him.

His gruff answer was simply, "You made the wrong choice."

He did not speak to her for days. Thereafter during their thirty-year marriage, during which George served several congregations, Margaret always checked with him before making even the most inconsequential decision.

"Why," I asked Margaret recently, "have you put up with it all these years?" "I couldn't stand ever again the awful silence and the look that could kill that I got for days after that 'wrong choice'. He says that the real strength in our marriage is my knowing whose judgments are right, and harkens back to the punch bowl episode as a key factor in our developing that "strength."

Rage and threat. So many hurting wives have identified these two eventual reactions to what began as relatively minor differences of opinion. Patterns of escalation from shouting to physical assault come out of nowhere in some cases; in others the hitting began even before marriage and continued. Of all the disturbing statistics which I have tried to digest and illustrate in this book, perhaps the most shocking was the discovery that in forty percent of all cases of wife assault, the first blow occurred *during pregnancy.*

Some men are like that

Sharon was pregnant with her third child. Her husband, Bob, had been an angry controller for most of their marriage, but had never struck her. It had never seemed all that bothersome to her; after all, she knew what he was like before the wedding. She had accepted "his ways" then, and had no one but herself to blame if the controlling behaviour had become a regular pattern.

So she was not ready for the first blow. Sharon and Bob were having an argument which he was "losing." He flew into a rage and hit her in the abdomen. Sharon had been carrying their baby for four months. The blow left an ugly bruise. Bob's nonchalant reaction to her obvious physical and emotional hurt was bad enough. But that did not prepare her for her doctor's remark the next day. After assuring her that there had been no fetal damage, he said "Some men are like that."[3] She fled his office, doubly dismayed.

Within a few years after the safe arrival of her child — and because Bob's worsening controlling behaviour deepened her fear of being struck again — Sharon declared that she wanted out of the marriage. Bob was thunderstruck. Family and friends — who didn't know *why* — were perplexed, and only years later did she explain her decision to her three equally perplexed teenaged children. Sharon's story is not unique. A medical researcher concludes a major study with these words:

> Pregnancy is a time when physical abuse often begins or escalates. Pregnant women are more likely to have multiple sites of injury than nonpregnant women, and are more likely to be struck on the abdomen.[4]

Sharon and her child were among the fortunate ones. The consequences of physical abuse during pregnancy range from missing appointments and neglecting prenatal care to serious hemorrhaging, hip dislocation or fractures, and miscarriage.

The saddest day of my life

Mabel and Charlie adopted a child, Charles Jr., whom they loved dearly and nourished into adulthood. Mabel never told him (or her friends) why she was unable to bear children although she and Charlie knew why. Recently, in a voice barely above a whisper, she told me the story of her one and only pregnancy.

After their marriage it was agreed that they would defer having a family until Charlie's business was established. The business would take a lot of energy, and besides it would be necessary for Mabel to have an income for the first few years in order to maintain a reasonably secure financial base.

A year into their marriage Mabel announced to Charlie that she was pregnant. She was happy beyond words. He trampled on her ecstasy by saying preemptively, "We cannot have this child." He flew into a rage, and gave Mabel a merciless tongue-lashing in which he accused her of tricking him into an "obviously" deliberate pregnancy. She cowered. He hounded her daily about going for an abortion. When it became apparent that she would not herself make the necessary arrangements, he marched her to their doctor's office and demanded an abortion. She was admitted to hospital, and at five and a half months pregnant, she had a damaging abortion which left her infertile.

And Charlie's reaction? Mabel told me recently, "He felt no distress at all, and never said he was sorry about what he had forced me to do. He did his thing in business, and became very prominent in the community and the church. He did enjoy running things — and people!"

Until his death some years ago, Mabel was always in mortal fear of Charlie. Yes, she loved Charles Jr., from whom she believes she concealed her fear of his father. But oh, how her heart ached for the child who might have been.

In a letter to me written in January 1994, Mabel has described the day of the forced abortion as "the saddest day of my life." She concludes,

> At what point do we capitulate our moral values? Or our theories, when it comes to living a good life? Or trying to make a marriage work? Where and when is the place for compromise in a marriage of allegiance — for one spouse to expose the other spouse to suspicion, danger, or disrepute? All of which happened to the wife of that marriage that many years ago.[5]

He hit me, so he must love me

Joan was marrying for a second time. During a premarriage counselling session she told me that her first husband, Gary, smacked her face during a minor disagreement before the wedding. She recalls thinking at the time, "That must mean that he loves me."

Three profound discussions with Joan and her fiancé, Phil, followed the disclosure. Shaking her head, she admitted that her thinking had been so distorted that she *knew* from that episode that they were meant to get married. From her present vantage point of restored dignity after a tortuous first marriage, Joan understands what froze her into silent acquiescence. The only times her father had expressed love for her mother — always with flowers — was after a beating episode. Affection and violence were so linked in little Joan's child-mind that when Gary hit her years later, she knew it was "love." It was years into the marriage before she discovered, with the help of a women's shelter advisor, that the association was toxic.

Yes, one blow should have been the last one. In fact it was only the first. Joan and Gary had two children. A final violent episode drove her over the threshold of tolerance; this time Joan feared for her life, and she and the children walked away. She saw to it that her children, who had often witnessed Gary's pattern of violence and remorse, had some therapeutic help to wash out that same toxicity and prepare them for their own marriages down the road.

If the cycle is not broken, however, family violence can become a permanent characteristic of the family itself. One woman describes her own family in this way:

> The more power [my husband] held over our heads the better. He'd seen his father do it to his mother. He'd seen his two other brothers do it to their wives and families. My husband had a scar on the back of his head, about two inches long, where his father had beaten him with a gun. And now, my sons do that to my daughters-in-law and their women ... [T]hey'd lock him up overnight, no charges, and send him home sober in the morning. The next day it would start again. I'd be pregnant in some cases, and I'd have miscarriages.[6]

I'll find you

One of the best known songs by the eighties group, The Police, was their hit, "Every Breath You Take." I heard the song often, but the words did not "sink in" until they were drawn to my attention recently:

Every breath you take
    every move you make
Every bond you break
    every step you take
I'll be watching you.

O can't you see
    you belong to me
How my poor heart aches
    with every step you take.

This is undeniably a "stalking song," but as recently as ten years ago lyrics like these in pop and country music were regarded as a somewhat innocent, even romantic expression of undying love — hardly offensive or criminal, and certainly not suggestive of possible homicide.

A male ownership model lies just below the surface of such lyrics as these. The issue is not really undying love, but unending *control.* The theme of stalking is also found in the biblical story of the destruction of Israel in the book of Lamentations. It describes pursuit by an enemy in a manner that echoes the fear and despair felt by women stalked by men who claim to love them:

They dogged our steps
    so that we could not walk in our streets;
our end drew near; our days were numbered;
    for our end had come.
Our pursuers were swifter
    than the eagles in the heavens;
they chased us on the mountains,
    they lay in wait for us in the wilderness. (4:18-19)

"I'll be watching you" or dogging the steps too often becomes a threat to harm. And because murder by a stalking husband or boyfriend has become such a dreadful reality, the Criminal Code of Canada was amended in 1993 to include it as a criminal offence. Although critics say the law does not go far enough to protect women, the act at least names the abuse and outlines penalties for those found guilty. It is commonly known as the "stalking law," although in the criminal code it is officially classified under "Criminal Harassment":

264. (1) No person shall, without lawful authority and knowing that another person is harassed or recklessly as to whether the other person is harassed, engage in conduct referred to in subsection (2) that causes that other person reasonably, in all the circumstances, to fear for their safety or the safety of anyone known to them.

(2) The conduct mentioned in subsection (1) consists of
(a) repeatedly following from place to place the other person or anyone known to them;
(b) repeatedly communicating with, either directly or indirectly, the other person or anyone known to them;
(c) besetting or watching the dwelling-house, or the place where the person, or anyone known to them, resides, works, carries on business or happens to be; or
(d) engaging in threatening conduct directed at the other person or any member of their family.

(3) Every person who contravenes this section is guilty of
(a) an indictable offence and is liable to imprisonment for a term not exceeding five years; or
(b) an offence punishable on summary conviction.

Other recent pieces of legislation are also relevant to "stalking": sections 372 ("False Messages") and 423 ("Intimidation").[7] All of these sections of the Criminal Code take cognizance of the *criminal* nature of verbal and psychological abuse. There is no guarantee that the law will be easy to enforce or that the rate of violence and murder will decline. Almost every night the local news still reports an instance of attempted or successful murder by a husband or a boyfriend.

I own you

One evening the CBC news carried a report of Peter, who had just been sentenced to a six-year penitentiary term for wounding his ex-girlfriend, Gladys. After she ended the relationship he declared that she had no right to do that. In his mind, he owned her. When Gladys refused his demand that she reconcile he threatened to stab her. With the help of friends he made arrangements to board a flight to London, England, immediately after the assault.

Peter stalked and stabbed Gladys, then was chauffeured to the airport. She survived the attack and, after being extradited from England for trial, Peter was found guilty on a wounding charge. He has since promised to "get her" upon release. In the CBC interview she said she could do little except carry on with her life in the hope that when he is paroled in about four years he will have "cooled off." Will the new provisions in the criminal code deter him? Gladys still has few options but to wait and see.

Living under a threat

Some years ago I was a participant in a Bible study group in which one of the members, Marie, indicated that her estranged husband, Grant, would be released from jail the following week. He was serving a short sentence in the local detention centre for assaulting her. While in jail Grant sent verbal messages to Marie that, upon release, he would "get her" for having blown the whistle on him.

The emphasis that evening shifted from the Bible to concern for Marie's safety. Had she asked for a restraining order or a peace bond? Had she formally indicated to the police that he was not to come near her? Yes, Marie assured us, these were written in as parole conditions. *By law*, he was not to harass her or come near her. But *in fact* she feared that he would make good his promise to hurt her. Not by coming to her home with advance notice, but by stalking her with violent intent.

The next week Marie came to the Bible study. We all breathed a sigh of relief. Yes, Grant was out on parole. No, he had made no attempt to contact her. Was he stalking her? She had no way of knowing. But the staff of a local shelter had given some advice on how to prevent, so far as possible, his interfering with her life (short of leaving town, which she was not going to do).

That was many years ago. Marie and Grant are now divorced. He is out of her life and has made no attempt to harass her. Marie is still safe. She lives day by day in the hope that he will fade completely from her life and never hurt her again.

Susan Tombolini never had a chance to do that. Early one morning in May 1993, her husband stalked her to the downtown Hamilton, Ontario, travel agency where she worked. He came up from behind her, pushed her to the ground in front of the agency, shot her in the head, and, as she lay dying on the sidewalk, he ambled up the street to the police station to turn himself in.

These recent incidents of stalking illustrate some common aftermaths of a decision to leave an abusive relationship. The hurting does not end with a walk or a court action.[8] Stalking has become so predictable that the threat of it is a heavy deterrent to a woman's desire to break free. There is now more community awareness about regarding stalking as a deadly serious offence; *finally* there are criminal sanctions against it. But it will continue to cast a menacing shadow over any woman who says "Enough!" and tries to leave the abuse behind.

Chapter 3

Marital Rape: "No" Still Means "No"

> On the seventh day, when the king was merry with wine, he commanded ... the seven eunuchs who attended him, to bring Queen Vashti before the king, wearing the royal crown, in order to show the peoples and the officials her beauty; for she was fair to behold. But Queen Vashti refused to come at the king's command conveyed by the eunuchs. At this the king was enraged, and his anger burned within him.... Then Memucan said in the presence of the king and the officials, "...this deed of the queen will be made known to all women, making them look with contempt on their husbands.... let it be written ... that Vashti is never again to come before King Ahasuerus ... he sent letters to all the royal provinces ... declaring that every man should be master in his own house.
>
> — from Esther 1:10-22

The command and subsequent rage of King Ahasuerus illustrate one form of abuse that shrouds the history of marriage — marital rape. Rape is any coerced sexual activity, against the will of the partner.

King Ahasuerus commanded Queen Vashti to parade her beauty (read "body") in public spectacle. She said "No," to this sexually exhibitionist act. The court advisor, Memucan, warned that, if she got away with it, all wives in the kingdom might model Vashti's impudence and start disobeying their husbands too. The king had better do something quickly to forestall such rebellion. Vashti was stripped of her royal prerogatives. A decree went out ordering all wives to remember their places and to *obey*, or else.

Sex as a duty

Sexual coercion in marriage starts as an attitude. "Anytime, anywhere," is the assumed sexual agenda for many husbands. Many women have been persuaded — either in their own homes as children, or in the general cultural milieu — to believe that submission to that agenda is part of the marriage package. In many family traditions, to demur, or to say "No" to one's husband, is tantamount to betrayal of the "commitment" to one another. Indeed, such submission might even be regarded as the surest sign of a woman's love for her husband.[1]

Some of the traditional discourse around marriage does suggest that a wife is obliged to accept her husband's "anytime, anywhere" mind-set. We speak of a wife "becoming one" with her husband. If this evident loss of identity is combined with her assuming his surname, then it is not a big jump to the conclusion that marriage puts her body under his jurisdiction as well. In short, "I do" has often been taken as permanent consent to sex.

If you think that "submission" is too strong a word, then let me tell you an "among women" secret. Since I have devoted so much of my thinking and writing to women's issues in the past several years, women have chosen to share with me some insider views that just never come up in mixed company. I have been told several times that many women look forward to their menstrual period as a time when they may have "justified" respite from a husband's sexual insistence. This does not in the least imply an overall lack of sexual desire of the wife's part. Neither does it imply that sexual desire and physical intimacy shut down during menstruation. What it does imply is another kind of desire, namely, to be sexually intimate with her husband *when she wants to*, and not only in response to his own romantic stimulation. Most men, alas, are "hurt" if their advances are not successful. The timing, variety, and frequency of sexual intimacy, in other words, should come from shared decisions.

Of course, there will be times when one will want intimacy and the other not; flirting and courtship will sometimes be a "fun" part of any marriage. Being "turned on" after initial apathy will occasionally be part of healthy sexuality. But we are speaking here of overall patterns of intimacy, where a husband assumes, without any further discussion, that the sexual agendas in the marriage are his prerogative.

The term "marital rape" is increasingly being used to flag both coerced sexual activity and violent sexual activity within marriage. Most pastoral counsellors or friends to whom a wife might disclose violent sexuality would undoubtedly label it as a form of rape. But few would regard coerced marital "intimacy" as rape: for many the expression is simply a contradiction in terms. The very word "rape" is the problem, I think. Usually it has been used to describe unwanted sexual *attack* by a stranger, which suggests violence. But unwanted intimacy — violent or not — is still rape. Forcing one's wife into sex against her will is *emotionally violent.* For women who have experienced such coercion within marriage, the damage is severe.[2]

Physically violent marital sexuality is more prevalent than we would like to believe. In one study,[3] one woman in ten reported that she had been forced sexually and physically by her husband. Furthermore, the fact that the assailant was one's husband did not reduce the long-range trauma and the blow to one's sense of dignity. Forcing one's wife is just that — an indignity. To demand such "intimacy" of one's wife is to cut to ribbons any respect for the independence of mind which is essential to dignity. It is also not possible to achieve real "intimacy" when one of the partners is forced or "persuaded." Intimacy is only achieved by mutual consent.

Coerced sexual acts other than intercourse are reported more frequently in our "try anything" age. The typical coerced sexual act described in the survey mentioned above was anal intercourse. Fellatio and cunnilingus are frequently included in contemporary portrayals of sexuality. While many couples do find mutual pleasure in oral sex, when a husband forcibly insists on something his wife finds offensive, then it is a form of rape.

It is difficult enough to write of such instances of sexual abuse, and even more so to discuss them. Few wives are willing to label such unwanted sexual activity as abuse — partly because the "intimacy climate" suggests that in modern marriage "anything goes." Yet there can be little doubt that a sense of being less "sexy" than her husband wants her to be — and thinks he deserves — and compromising her own values around body intimacy in the interests of "giving in" contribute to a loss of self-esteem.

You always cried, Mummy

During the writing of this book a number of people were intrigued by its title, and invariably asked what was its subject matter. "Wife abuse? Oh." Long pause. Some of the stories, including this one, were told after such a pause.

Beatrice had been divorced from Archie for three years, and was raising twelve-year old Tracy on her own. Tracy had entered puberty six months before, and had been quiet and withdrawn ever since. She kept to her room a lot, and discouraged friends from coming to visit. "What's wrong?" Beatrice had asked persistently, to which Tracy always replied, "Nuthin." Tracy had been a willing listener when Beatrice told her about puberty, and had expressed no anxiety about her new menstrual experience. So Beatrice was perplexed: why the change?

One day the first clue came out at the breakfast table. Tracy muttered almost inaudibly, "It hurt, didn't it." Beatrice didn't get it. "What hurt?"

Tracy replied, "You always cried after Daddy got up. Now I know what you were doing. And you cried and cried after Daddy got up; I could hear you, and I was so scared. You always cried, Mummy, so it must have hurt."

Yes, Beatrice remembered. And over the next months she explained that the way Daddy forced himself on her night after night — roughly, almost savagely — did hurt. Her cries were from the physical pain of forced, dry entry, but even more from the degradation she felt in being used. She was never caressed, never spoken to with endearments. And, yes, she did cry afterwards.

Beatrice and Tracy are still talking about ways in which sexual intimacy need not be rough. For both it is theoretical. Beatrice never wanted to date another man again after the divorce. Tracy fears her first sexual contact. Mother and daughter may enter into therapy together, and separately. Rape in marriage has cast an ugly shadow over both their lives.

It is vital to identify marital sexual coercion for what it is — rapacious abuse. There is no justification for a "husband's sexual prerogative" in a marriage. But such a view is so embedded in the general culture that it will be difficult to persuade men that it is abusive to insist on sex when the other partner does not consent. Without a shift in the collective mind-set we shall continue to be deluded into believing that "abuse means bruises." Not so. There are bruises of the soul that can't be seen and that destroy dignity.

The "fallen woman" syndrome

Sadly, it must be pointed out that the "male prerogative" view of marital sexuality is biblically entrenched. Even though adultery was committed by both men and women, generally only women were punished, often by death. If a man was dissatisfied with his wife, he could issue her a certificate of divorce, but a woman could not take the same initiative (Deuteronomy 24:1). If a woman was raped, she was too "unclean" to marry anyone else and was forced to marry the rapist (Exodus 22:16). If a man suspected his bride of not being a virgin and the charge was shown to be false, then he had to pay a fine of one hundred shekels to the accused woman's father.

> If, however, this charge is true, that evidence of the young woman's virginity was not found, then they shall bring the young woman out to the entrance of her father's house and the men of the town shall stone her to death, because she committed a disgraceful act in Israel by prostituting herself in her father's house. So you shall purge the evil from your midst.
>
> — DEUTERONOMY 22:20-21

The truth is that the Bible does not have a full-blown and consistent theology of marriage. The sixty-six books which make up this "library" (the meaning of the word "Bible") reflect a diversity of cultures over a time period from roughly two thousand B.C. to one hundred A.D. The references given above do not, therefore, represent the "biblical" view of male sexual dominance, with the correlative principles of female virginity. It would be a mistake to derive an ethic of marriage from the Bible alone, and equally so to portray the sanctions indicated as general practice for over two thousand years.

Just as Canada has a justice system that has developed over many centuries, based on British common law and the French civil code, so too have we struggled toward a marriage ethic by taking account of the ideas of many women and men since Christ. The freedom even to discuss marriage intimacy was relatively unheard of before Freud. In the century since he wrote we have been helped by a vast medical, psychiatric, and theological literature to arrive at views of personal relationships in which mental health and individual fulfillment have replaced child bearing as among the "reasons" for marriage.

In biblical times the purpose of marriage was to guarantee the survival of the race by producing children. In patriarchal society, women and children were seen as the property of the male head of the household. It was important to pass one's property on through one's sons in order to preserve the male line. In such societies it was also necessary to control women's sexuality to ensure that offspring produced "belonged" to the husband. Virginity, chastity, and fidelity of wives were therefore essential to preserving male power and inheritance. Sanctions against women who transgressed the sexual boundaries of patriarchy, or even women who were victims of rape, incest or other male abuse, were severe and often deadly. In short, the woman's womb, along with the rest of her body, was her husband's property.

Little is ever said of tender marriage intimacy; euphemisms like "knew" and "lay with" are *always* male-as-subject, female-as-object. Is it any wonder that in the overall cultural view — undergirded by patriarchal biblical authority — husbands assume that they drive the sexual agenda for marriage?

Marriage as a sexual partnership

Two biblical scenarios that do show an egalitarian male-female sexuality can be found, however, neither one deals with marriage. They are quoted frequently to illustrate tender rather than exploitative sexuality.

In the prose poem "The Song of Songs" sexual intimacy is lyrically portrayed between two betrothed in non-genital terms. The lovers run toward one another (2:8-9), they delight in seeing and hearing each other (2:14, 7:10), and they want nothing more than to please each other (8:1-3). The poem is virtually non-patriarchal, and the initiator is sometimes male, sometimes female. The poem is an oasis of sexual tenderness in a Bible that is often anything but tender in its accounts of sexuality.

The other instance of non-exploitative intimacy, in this case initiated by a woman, occurs in the Gospel of John:

> Six days before the Passover Jesus came to Bethany, the home of Lazarus, whom he had raised from the dead. There they gave a dinner for him. Martha served, and Lazarus was one of those at the table with him. Mary took a pound of costly perfume made of pure nard, anointed Jesus' feet, and wiped them with her hair. The house was filled with the fragrance of the perfume. (12:1-3)

Jesus and Mary were not husband and wife. There is no suggestion that their intimacy went beyond the touching described in the gospel. Some prefer to see the story as totally devoid of sexual content, based on a resistance to any thought of Jesus having a sensual nature. A similar repugnance prevents many from appreciating such movies as *Jesus Christ, Superstar* and *The Last Temptation of Christ* as helpful to an understanding of Jesus.

But for me the story of Mary and Jesus is sensuous in the best possible meaning of the term, and towers above all other portrayals of the male-female relationship in the Bible. Yes, Mary is shown as serving Jesus, but the simple desire to *give* pleasure rather than to *take* pleasure is the essence of mutually agreeable sexuality. It represents somehow the very antithesis of the undignified and rapacious sexuality expressed in so many other biblical accounts. It suggests an image of what God had in mind in creating women and men to be partners — dignity, tenderness, generosity, pleasure, and adoration.

Chapter 4

Damaged Children: Violence Begets Violence

> The parents have eaten sour grapes, and the children's teeth are set on edge.
>
> — Ezekiel 18:2

In 1992 I took part in a one-day workshop on caring for children who need help and counselling. The focus was on children who were being physically hurt — by incest or by physical beatings. But there was also discussion of the emotional hurt of living in a violent home and the pain of seeing violence, which, ominously, would likely be repeated in their own patterns of parenting down the road. There were a number of teachers at the workshop, and they helped us to think about ways that we could reach out in friendship to children who seemed burdened, sad, humourless.

Since we tend to think of children as maleable creatures, sometimes adults forget that permanent damage can be inflicted with harsh words and environments. We learned that it was important to let little ones know that "family" would eventually include non-shouters and non-hurters, and that to interfere even slightly with the cycle of violence was worth the effort. Studies have shown, in fact, that adults outside the nuclear family — a grandparent, aunt or uncle, Scout or Guide leader, minister, teacher or guidance counsellor, for example — can help an endangered child grow into a thriving adult, simply by providing an outlet from and a counterbalance to a troubled home.[1]

In many families, the nuclear family can be a pressure cooker of tension. In the film *The Prince of Tides*, the main character describes such suffocating family relations in these words: "I don't know when my parents began their war against each other, but I do know that their only prisoners were their children."[2]

I was four years old

"I was four years old. Mom heard Dad yelling as he stumbled up the porch steps. He was drunk, as usual. She was going crazy trying to look after us kids with almost no money. Anyway, she was so fed up this time that she grabbed two twenty-sixers from the cupboard and was pouring them down the sink just as Dad came in the door. He saw what she was doing, went up to her, and broke both her arms."

Danny muttered the words so low you could hardly hear him. He was a participant in a male Addictions Rap Group at the Hamilton-Wentworth Detention Centre. Bruce Taylor and I co-facilitated the group on the fourth level of the Detention Centre. Bruce was a "rounder": he had served penitentiary time, was a recovered alcoholic, and a long-time member of AA. I was a "square john": I had never been in jail, was not addicted, and was as straight as they come. Every member of the group was on the fourth level — high security — for having violated federal parole or awaiting trial on a charge involving some form of violence.

Bruce had walked their walk, and could talk their talk. He knew their angers, their vulnerabilities, and particularly their denial strategies. I had led discussion groups in church, labour union, and university settings for twenty-five years, so knew my way around "process." Bruce and I had been friends for about twelve years, and received authorization from the Centre to conduct the group every Monday evening. We thought that the combination of our histories and skills might help some inmates to a glimpse of self-awareness.

Before our first session Bruce gave me a tip. "Don't ask the guy what his beef is, or how he broke parole. Just ask when he first drank to get drunk."

Danny had been to the group a few times before, so he knew that Bruce couldn't be conned and that I was a well-meaning but likely naive Rev. I asked him, "Danny, when did you first drink to get drunk?"

"Thirteen."

Silence. Not a word was said by any of the half-dozen men who were there. Then, so quietly he could hardly be heard, Danny went on, "I... ah, saw a lot of boozing at home." Silence again. "I drank to be like my dad." Silence. Then, "I was four years old...."

We learned later that Danny was awaiting trial on a number of assault charges. He was drunk each time.

I am my fists

Over the years of our friendship Bruce had told me his childhood story as a street tough in the Little Norway section of Toronto. From his earliest years he thieved, scrapped, used and sold pills, and was clearly on his way to a career in crime. He was to serve a total of six years in maximum security provincial and federal correctional facilities; his first incarceration was at the age of nine.

"And home and the neighbourhood? What was it like?"

"Violent. Most of the families were stressed out, and on the streets kids fought and stole. My older brother's job was to discipline me, and that meant getting hit — a lot. He used to beat on me and Dad was always beating on Mom. I mean heavy. I ran with a gang of kids who stole what we could whenever we could. I was learning that you survived by being tough, and in my first prison sentence at Millbrook (a maximum security provincial correctional centre) I found out that if you could win fights you were left alone."[3]

Bruce is now the Director of a residential treatment facility for addicted persons. Over the years he has heard the stories of many men and women who, like himself, were raised in violent, unpredictable environments. He has confessed to me that learning to live by your fists does not stop when you "grow up" and have a family. He had been physically abusive to his wife while he was drinking, but even after joining AA he continued to strike her. By then he and I were becoming close friends; my first lesson in the "cycle of violence" was when he told me that the urge to hit was built into him. This is a self-definition that, as a philosopher, I had certainly never heard before: "I am my fists."

Bruce has helped me to understand some of the crooked patterns of thinking which drive men to abuse their wives. He acknowledges with genuine shame his abusive history. At AA meetings and in men's workshops, which we still co-lead, he speaks forcefully about those crooked patterns, and of how perilous they become when mixed with alcohol.

Men, in general, are reluctant to speak of painful memories of childhood; abusive men in particular don't want to speak of childhood hurts. Men like Danny are sometimes freed up enough to speak in prison discussion or "anger control" groups, but only after a deep enough level of trust has been established. Abusive men are usually macho as well — wearing a tough guy false face and going to any lengths to conceal vulnerability from others. In my own experience, abusive men have *always* had a history of childhood abuse. Empty holes of childhood neglect are puttied over by years of a type of bravado which can easily become violent.

Because of this clearly demonstrated connection, I relate two stories — one about Tommy, who will almost certainly become an abusive man, and the other about Tom, aged forty-three, in whom a wounded "Tommy" still resides.

The concentric scars

Tommy's pre-kindergarten teacher, Evelyn, first noticed the concentric scars. He had been absent from school for about three weeks for "medical reasons." The bandages were still on when he returned to class, but there was something else. He had been a playful and talkative little guy before, but now he would not speak. He always held his head down, and refused to play with the other children. The day I met him he was sitting by himself, listlessly playing with a toy fire station. His teacher had told me of his changed behaviour, and since I had planned to visit her class sometime anyway, she suggested that this was a good time, and that I might want to sit on the floor beside Tommy.

When I knelt down, he raised his eyes once, and not again during the five minutes I was beside him. I backed a firetruck out of the station, and asked if he would push the little siren button. Still keeping his head down, and without a trace of a smile, he pushed the siren, held it down for a few seconds, then sat motionless.

Evelyn had told me to look at the front of Tommy's left arm. It had four deep concentric scars. The "medical reason" for his absence from school had been that he'd accidentally brushed his arm against a hot-plate. The question of why he continued to hold his arm on the hot-plate long enough to cause deep burns had been dismissed by the family, and was left unexamined by their doctor: "Tommy often did things to extremes," they'd said. "But," Evelyn said, "a Board [of Education] social worker has seen him and talked to the family. Though his parents deny any deliberate hurting in this case, it did come out that Tommy was often a bad boy, and had to be physically punished."

"Mort," Evelyn continued, "Tommy's hand was *held down* on the rings of that hot-plate. We cannot prove it. The social worker and I are so angry.... But nothing can be done."

Three months later Evelyn reported, "Tommy has remained mute, and has started to hit girls. By the time he's twelve, he'll be a holy terror. And when he marries, without any doubt he'll hurt his wife. To punish her. I know it."

That was several years ago. I recently asked Evelyn how Tommy was doing. She told me that he now speaks and is doing moderately well in the upper grades, but is already notorious for hitting people without the slightest provocation. Girls stay away from him. And Evelyn believes even more firmly than ever that he will most certainly be an abusive adult. The patterns of bullying and intimidation Tommy was trying to inflict on his classmates were, without a doubt, the same ones that he had learned at home.

Tom, forty-three, has been physically abusive in two marriages and is currently serving an eight-year sentence in Kingston Penitentiary for armed robbery. I first met him when he was a teenager — a handsome, articulate, and winsome young man. I could not fathom his negative self-image, and it was only after speaking with his newly adoptive parents that I discovered the reason. Tom had been in ten foster homes between the ages of two and twelve since being removed from his birth home by the Children's Aid Society. When he was two he had been beaten into unconsiousness by his mother — with a lead pipe.

I later learned that what I had seen as winsomeness was a carefully crafted mechanism for drawing people close to him in order to hurt them. This became a *modus vivendi*, a life pattern which inevitably culminated in his hurting a woman or committing a crime with a weapon.

Why am I speaking of Tommy and Tom in the same discussion of childhood hurt? Because Tommy grows into Tom. In men's groups and in private conversation I have yet to meet a physically abusive man who wasn't traumatized as a boy. This is not to excuse or exhonerate. It is not to say "what can you expect?" as a way of dismissing the problem. It *is* to say that a good deal of male abusive behaviour is predictable from an early age.

Raise this issue with any kindergarten teacher, and she or he will surely tell you of children sitting in silence and raging within. Self-worth was burned out of Tommy by an act of torture, and part of his response is to attack someone else's dignity. The importance of restoring the dignity of a child cannot be overemphasized. To do so for a boy is the best way to *prevent* the development of a violent man. And to help a girl keep a sense of pride and dignity will enable her to say "No" to abuse of any kind — because she knows women deserve better.

Can you keep a secret?

It may have seemed innocent enough at the time to her parents. They probably would have been shocked to know that they were inflicting emotional abuse on their only child, yet abuse takes many forms. Janet was made the bearer of family secrets when she was just a preschooler. Each parent told her bits of information about the other and about the ways in which they were being wronged or misunderstood. "Now don't let on you know this," they always warned, with unstated dire consequences if Janet "told." Often there was a rider to the secret, a question: "What do you think I should do?"

Janet cannot remember a time when she was not both parents' confidant, and looks back to a childhood burdened by too much knowledge. There was always a pall over the most ordinary of mealtime conversations, with just a hint of intrigue. Each parent would speak with enough innuendo to make it clear to Janet that the secrets gave her a privileged position of power. But the power and the knowledge were both unwelcome. Janet remembers a childhood without frivolity; a weighed-down childhood of being a parent to each parent.[4]

Janet has recaptured some of the glee of childhood by becoming a "child-like" adult — open, adventurous, and spontaneous. She entered into private therapy to try to unburden herself of some of the weights which she still carried, and found it liberating. Now that she is an adult she has some power to change the pattern and refuse to harbour painful secrets any longer. As a woman approaching middle-age, there is still much that she wants to explore in therapy, including getting, and staying, in touch with the little girl inside.

Nothing seems funny

Gord too is middle-aged, also trying to find "Gordie" within. The first impression one gets of him is of a serious, but on the whole "together" individual. In conversation one day soon after we had met, I made a remark that I thought was amusing, though I've been known to overestimate my comic abilities. Gord didn't laugh. "Okay," I thought to myself, "it wasn't all that funny, or Gord's having a bad day, or both." Then he said, "You know, believe it or not, nothing seems funny to me. If something is said that other people laugh at, I pretend to laugh. But my wife knows that it's not real. She's tried to help me, and I see a psychiatrist for some depression that hangs on. He can't figure it out either. He doesn't think it would do me too much good to delve into my past; his approach is clinical, and we're trying to find the right combination of medications. Anyway, I don't really want to get into my past either. It makes me sad."

"Well, Gord," I said, "I'm not a psychiatrist, and I won't try to go against his treatment. But let's just talk as friends, okay?"

"Sure," he replied, unsmiling.

"Wasn't anything funny as a kid? Didn't you have snowball fights, or laugh at the crokinole table, or dress up crazy at Hallowe'en?"

"Nope."

"What was it like at home?"

"I don't really want to get into it, Mort. But I will say that my mother and father were always at it. There weren't many days that he wasn't telling her to shut up, and if any of us kids crossed him, he sure belted us."

"Mum. Tell me about her, Gord. If you feel like it."

"Mum? We never called her that. Only Mother. Not much to say. She was kind of... there, not much more. My father was always correcting her. She never said much. Boy, she was a good cook. All I remember is that we never had fun. You know, I can hardly remember much about my mother. Strange, eh?"

"Know what.... why don't we go to some kid's movies — just for fun. What do you say?"

"Why not. I wonder if Pete would come with us?"

Pete was a mutual friend who also knew about Gord's dead seriousness. We had remarked to each other how much of life Gord was missing by seeing nothing funny. The three of us began to see children's movies together: *Hook, Beethoven, Aladdin.* Gord caught himself chuckling at times. Not guffaws. But he was having fun. Pete, Gord and I still go to movies together. Kid's movies.

When it comes right down to it, the questions are these: Do parents own their children? Does "anything go" behind the walls of home? Is it really okay if a child is always frightened? And if it was like that for you as a child, ask yourself this tough question: Is *your* home a place of fun and laughter or does each member of your family find real fun somewhere else?

PART II

RESPONSE

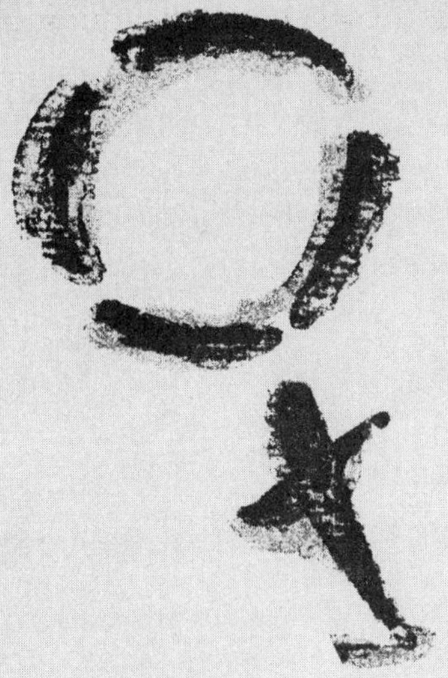

If you do abuse them, when they cry out to me, I will surely heed their cry; my wrath will burn...

— EXODUS 22:23-24a

Chapter 5
Hot Caring

> Now our flesh is the same as that of our kindred; our children are the same as their children; and yet we are forcing our sons and daughters to be slaves, and some of our daughters have been ravished;[1] we are powerless, and our fields and vineyards now belong to others. I was very angry when I heard their outcry and these complaints. After thinking it over, I brought charges against the nobles and the officials.
>
> — NEHEMIAH 5:5-7A

Nehemiah reacted with hot anger at the news that there were great inequities between rich and poor in Jerusalem. There was famine. Some were starving. Many were going into debt. Nehemiah was governor of Jerusalem, which then, as for most of its history, was under foreign rule. This time it was Persia which ruled Jerusalem. Artaxerxes, a benign king, gave Nehemiah permission to coordinate Jews who lived in the city in a massive reconstruction project, mainly the rebuilding of the city wall. But it wasn't long before inequities developed within the Jewish population. Before they had all been subservient to the foreign king, but now some Jews were subjugating others, and women were being raped by fellow citizens.

In anger, Nehemiah brought charges against those responsible. The inequities and the sexual domination of women were so intolerable that he charged the nobles and officials who had allowed the practices, and insisted that they stop.

The Hebrew verb *charah* means both "to burn" and "to be angry." Cain was angry at Abel — angry enough to kill. God asked him "*lammah charah*?" or "Why are you angry?" Literally, God was asking "Why are you burning?"

We often use a similar epithet, saying of someone who is extremely angry that "she's burning," or "he's really hot." "Hot Caring," the title of this chapter, draws attention to another epithetical use of the notion of heat — caring. Before there can be such hot caring for victims of woman abuse, there has to be hot anger. If you aren't *angry* enough to care, then you won't care. The kind of caring we are speaking about is fuelled by the same coals as anger.

It is one thing for a woman to *know* that she is being manipulated, demeaned, struck, or sexually coerced by her husband. It is another step for her to *do* something about it. It is one thing for men to *know* that one woman in four is being or has been abused by her present or former husband, quite another to *do* something about it.

The motivation is *anger.* If a woman who is being hurt at home stifles feelings of rage, or regards such feelings as illegitimate, then she will likely continue to tolerate the abuse. Women have not generally been given cultural "permission" to express anger, so there is a built-in block to expressing it or acting on it. For a woman being hurt at home, anger can be the heat which lets her care for *herself.* Hot caring.

Men who are blasé about the severity and extent of woman abuse will have little or no motivating anger to effect changes, especially in their own behaviour. The relative male disinterest concerning the mental, physical, and sexual abuse of women in the community can be traced, I believe, to an inability and/or a refusal to get hot enough to make radical changes. Men, and I include myself, stand indicted. But we *can* change. We *can* get blazing mad, and *do* something. There is a Nehemiah inside each one of us, and only heat will let him out. Hot caring.

There are several cultural reasons why both men and women have trouble expressing anger. Let's start with religion. Most of us like our religion calm and unprovocative. If asked, "What is the main consequence of faith?" most would answer with something like "peace of mind." In the areas of both personal growth and interpersonal relations we have become accustomed to hearing that faith in God and friendship with Jesus help one to be fully and happily human. Faith brings inner harmony and a positive outlook in the face of life's vicissitudes. God's love is "patient and kind, not irritable or resentful, bears all things, believes all things, hopes all things, endures all things" (from I Corinthians 13:4-7). Love is the highest Christian virtue. In the ideal Christian life such divinely inspired love is expressed in our human relationships — most directly within the family.

Peace of mind is a marvellous consequence of faith, but it is not always appropriate. Love for God and for one another is the greatest virtue, and I shall continue to read those words from I Corinthians 13 at weddings. But problems arise if one is led to believe that any emotion that does not incline towards peace of mind and the expression of love is somehow wrong and out of place.

Like anger. Being angry at God or at one another seems patently wrong. If one assumes that anger is contrary to love, then it must always seem unloving. This simple belief has led to a lot of grief. It has blocked the expression of legitimate, "good" anger. It is a block which prevents honest communication of how one feels, and is nowhere more destructive than when a woman is abused, and she feels she should contain her anger. For the teaching of the church has so often been "to endure"[2] — to keep angry thoughts under control.

Female anger is frequently discounted as "proof" of an over-emotional nature. Put downs such as "The kids must have gotten to you today," or "It must be your time of the month," rather than any admission of fault by the husband are common. The eminent psychotherapist, Harriet Lerner, says of male denial in *The Dance of Anger*:

> When a woman shows her anger, she is likely to be dismissed as irrational or worse. At a professional conference I attended recently, a young doctor presented a paper about battered women. She shared many new and exciting ideas and conveyed a deep and personal involvement in her subject. In the middle of her presentation, a well-known psychiatrist who was seated behind me got up to leave. As he stood, he turned to the man next to him and made his diagnostic pronouncement: "Now that is a very angry woman." That was that! The fact that he detected — or thought he detected — an angry tone to her voice disqualified not only

> what she had to say but also who she was. Because the very possibility that we are angry often meets with rejection and disapproval from others, it is no wonder that it is hard for us to know, let alone admit, that we are angry.[3]

There is a third complication when it comes to expressing anger. Not only do we feel that our faith doesn't allow it. Not only do men typically try to throw an angry wife off balance by a snide put-down. The real difficulty is that few of us were ever taught how to deal with anger — our own or someone else's. Most of us have trouble handling anger because as children we were taught that it was a no-no, part of a range of "negative" emotions that were not to be displayed. It was often not clear whether it was the having or the expressing of those emotions that was somehow wrong. So if we were upset at something said or done to us, it was kept inside, buried behind a facade of resentful silence.

Furthermore, many of us may have witnessed the expression of adult anger as something fearful — frightening scenes of raised voices and thrown objects or the vague but threatening closure of "not in front of the children." Rare is the home where children witness their parents argue in constructive and loving ways.

I'm so angry I could kill!

Cindy is the mother of two active pre-school children. After spending the whole day alone with them, her nerves are frayed. When Lloyd gets home from work, rather than romp with them for a while to give Cindy a chance to lie down, he clutches his evening paper and sinks into his favorite chair; he has to relax after a hard day at the office.

On one occasion Brian, the younger of the two live-wires, did what experience should have taught him not to do. In an attempt to get some attention, he began to pester his dad by hitting the spread-out newspaper. Lloyd folded the paper, gave Brian a back-hander that sent him sprawling, picked up the paper again, and resumed his reading.

But not without an emotional back-hander for Cindy as well: "Do something with these brats? Can't you see I'm trying to wind down?" Cindy kept quiet. She didn't want to annoy Lloyd further.

Her job, she thought, was to keep the peace and to ensure a calm home for her poor frazzled husband.

She asked to speak with me one day after church. Lloyd's husbandly concession was to stay home from the golf course on Sunday mornings ("too many duffers out there, anyway") to look after "the brats." Cindy escaped to the Eden-like peace and quiet of the church service. In my office she spoke with frustration and with obvious fear of what she was capable of doing.

"It's getting to me. He never helps look after them. Some days I'm so beside myself that I could kill one or both of the kids! I'm on medication, which helps. It's not them I'm angry at; it's Lloyd, but I don't dare say anything to him. He'd get so cross. But he does work awfully hard, and when I think about it, I realize how lucky I am; at least there's a paycheque every week. And he's never hit me — only the kids."

Cindy's steadily mounting anger at the children was certainly aimed at the wrong target, but she was able to identify how unfair this was before it resulted in tragedy.[4]

There was no point in trying to change Lloyd. As Lerner points out, it is a fantasy that a woman can change her husband. But she could use "that same anger energy to clarify her choices and take new actions on her own behalf."[5] Cindy did begin to use that "anger energy" to develop a network of women who visited her and gave her respite care now and again while she went for a walk or did some shopping. She admitted that her anger was always there and could get out of hand. They became a support team "cheering her on."

The youngest woman in the group suggested the idea of "I-statements"[6] which she had heard about in a recent pre-marital counselling course. The more Cindy talked about her feelings, the more "in control" she felt. She was able to stop taking the medication — "nerve pills" she called them — and even began to tell Lloyd when she was angry.

Lloyd's behaviour didn't change. He continued to play virtually no role in raising the children. He was an absent father and an increasingly critical husband. But he had his own relief valves; he played golf to a 5 handicap in the summer (to keep it at 5 he had to play three times a week, he said) and curled regularly all winter.

Cindy suggested marriage counselling but Lloyd rejected the idea out of hand: "There's nothing wrong with our marriage, and besides where would I find the time?" But rather than being exasperated by his patronizing denial, Cindy began personal marriage counselling — for her own sake. After a month she decided on a temporary marital separation, and when Lloyd laughed heartily at the proposal ("Where would you be without me, kiddo?"), she and her "cheerleaders" began looking for a place she could stay and when she found one she moved out.

By the way, the children did fine despite the separation. Yes, some days are still frantic. But instead of jumping up and down in a tantrum when they are upset, they have learned from Mum how to "say" they are angry.

I-statements

An I-statement describes how one feels. A you-statement describes what another person has done. One is expressive, the other is accusatory. In an argument with Lloyd, Cindy might say, "All you do when you come home from work is read your paper." Or she could say, "I am angry that you come home and don't help with the kids; I'm tired too, you know."

The difference seems minimal, but it is crucial. An I-statement expresses a feeling, and is not open to contradiction. If Cindy says, "I'm angry," it would be difficult for Lloyd to reply, "No, you're not." He might answer with a prickly "You have no reason to be angry," or even "You were angry last night too." But the initial response would likely be something like, "Oh!" or "Why?"

Communication has a better chance of staying open if accusations are not made about the other person's behaviour. An accusatory you-statement begs for defensive rebuttal. A self-disclosing I-statement at worst invites snide commentary, at best a request for clarification.

The difference can be illustrated by a brief conversation I had with a close friend not long ago. Right out of the blue, but very calmly, he said to me, "You know, Mort, I'm angry at you for something you did a year ago. I didn't know when would be a good time to tell you, but I think now is as good a time as any."

When I asked him to explain the situation that gave rise to his anger, he told me why. He wasn't agitated as he spoke, and the way he explained his anger was so courteous that I wasn't inclined to become the least bit defensive. I acknowledged that he had good reason to be angry, and apologized. The conversation returned to other matters. If anything his I-statement and the subsequent clarification deepened an already good friendship.

I have already introduced you to Bruce. Shortly after we met, an anger episode lifted us from being mere acquaintances into a friendship that has lasted over twenty years. We still look back to it as a turning point.

I had met Bruce in my role as a volunteer with the John Howard Society. He was a parolee. After joining AA, and through a deliberate commitment to association with "positive people," his change in life-style and attitude were astonishing. After a few short years he chaired the John Howard Board. Visiting in our home one evening, he spoke of his childhood, his highs and his lows, his gains and his losses, and especially what it meant to him now to be in a position of trust. He was flying high, but his monologue was devoid of any reference to ways in which his wife and family had encouraged him. Nor did he include them in his ecstasy.

I grew restless, then urged him to stop talking. I said I was angry; we'd heard lots about Bruce but nothing about his family supports. Would he please tell my wife and me something about his wife and children. As he told me later, he was incensed at what he saw as a stern put-down. So seldom in his life had he done things right. Now he was. And what he needed at that point was recognition, not criticism.

There was a moment's silence. Then he leapt from his chair, jammed on his jacket, and stomped to the door. As he slammed it he shouted, "Well you can go to hell!" He intended never to speak to me again.

The next day he telephoned me at my office. "Let's talk," he said. We met later in the day for coffee. I forgot what we talked about. It doesn't really matter. My angry I-statement — which surprised both of us — his hot response, and our quick return to converstation were the foundation of a years-long friendship. Some fifteen years later, we agree that without that hot exchange, it is doubtful that we would have become friends.

We've been talking about the expressing of one's *own* anger in ways that are energizing or creative. Clearly anger need not be regarded as a negative, draining emotion, but can be the stimulus to personal and interpersonal change.

In Cindy's case, anger ignited a drive toward a strong sense of self and control over her own destiny. By articulating and identifying her fear that she could hurt her children, she started the process of letting her anger at Lloyd's attitudes and behaviour work *for* her instead of *against* her. She recognized that her anger toward the children was misplaced or "wrong-target" anger, and that it could only be destructive.

My friend's decision that "now" was the time to say that he was angry with me, and my own spur-of-the-moment I-statement to Bruce, released energy for the subsequent deepening of friendships.

God's Anger

In the Bible the target of God's anger is usually the covenant people. A covenant is an agreement that two parties will abide by certain conditions that will govern their relationship. The terms of that husband/wife covenant between God and the people of Israel were outlined in Chapter 1. Even though we saw it a one-sided decision on God's part as to what the terms of the covenant would be, it was nonetheless a strong model of how God and created humanity might relate.

Two Hebrew terms are used to describe God's reaction to Israel's breaking of covenant — both of which are derived from "hot." One is *'esh*, and literally means "fire." It is usually translated "wrath," a term which is now out of fashion. But the use of *'esh* as a metaphor shows vividly the depth of divine disappointment that covenant has been broken. The other word, already mentioned at the beginning of this chapter, is *charon*, which comes from a verb meaning "to burn." The anger which is mentioned in the two passages at the head of this part and of this chapter (Exodus 22:23-24a and Nehemiah 5:5-7a) are both *charon* anger. In the second passage it is Nehemiah's. In the first it is God's.

God's *'esh* (wrath) or *charon* (anger) are white hot. We might want to soften the descriptions, and join that wide class of Christians for whom God is always "nice" and for whom religion is always "positive." Admittedly, to speak of God in human terms is metaphorical in any case, but we *do* believe that, in ways beyond our imaginings, God loves and cares. Does God always "care" nicely, or is there a caring which contains anger?

God's wrath *is* enflamed with the breaking of the covenant; the breaking of trust; the waywardness of the people Israel in seeking other gods. These all drew from God an intensity of anger which could only be described as hot. It was an anger mixed with tears of discouragement, but the depth of the hurt was such that only profound anger could match it.

Now we ask the question again of a woman who has been abused, for whom the covenant of marriage was broken by deliberate hurting. One marries with the expectation that there will be mutually supportive "cheering." And if the expectation is not met — if cheering has become jeering, whether emotional, physical or sexual — then the covenant has been broken. It is no longer a question of the abused one wondering whether she should "break the vow" and leave because the vow has already been broken *de facto.* Her question now is, will I allow myself the anger that is justified?

I have spoken with hurting wives who could not for the life of them permit the anger within to explode. Instead it "implodes," so women — not the abusers — bear the brunt of their own justified anger. From so many directions — including the church — the message is: "It must be your fault if your husband is hurting you." To repeat the cruel question asked by the attending male emergency room physician in Tom Paxton's "She Sits on the Table," "What did you do to deserve such a beating as this?" For if the hurting was somehow brought on by herself, then obviously the one to be angry at is the victim. But again, this is "wrong-target" anger.

Now we return to Nehemiah's anger with some questions to men. Were you angry when I told you of Murray bringing his girlfriend into his wife's bed? Of Bob striking his pregnant wife? Of Charlie forcing his wife to abort their child? If you knew that Murray or Bob or Charlie sat in the next pew or lived on your street, would you get angry enough to do something about it?

Chapter 6

Wings Like a Dove

My heart is in anguish within me,
    the terrors of death have fallen upon me.
Fear and trembling come upon me,
    and horror overwhelms me.
And I say, "O that I had wings like a dove!
    I would fly away and be at rest;
truly I would flee far away;
    I would lodge in the wilderness;
I would hurry to find a shelter for myself
    from the raging wind and tempest"

— Psalm 55:4-8

"Until death do us part."

When are we going to wake up to the number of marriages for which this promise from the traditional wedding ceremony becomes a stark and mocking epitaph? Reports of domestic homicide are so widespread across the country that their sheer number escapes us.

We may be aware of the horrible massacre of fourteen women engineering students in Montreal on December 6th, 1989. What we may not know is that in the year following the Montreal massacre more than this number of wives were murdered by their husbands in that same city. Their blood was spilled on the carpets and beds of their own homes, and their names and the names of their executioners do not come to our attention or remain lodged in our minds.[1]

Earlier I tried to indicate some of the dynamics of those marriages in which a husband threatens to harm a wife who has left the marriage. Here I want to examine the flip side — where a wife who has been physically assaulted and even threatened with death stays, in part, because of her wedding vow never to leave. Because of her promise to stay ... till death.

This vow — or one similar to it — is said by the bride to her groom:

I take you to be my husband;
to laugh with you in joy,
to grieve with you in sorrow,
to grow with you in love,
to be faithful to you alone
as long as we both shall live.[2]

With whatever words the couple and the officiant agree upon, the promise is to honour, to cherish, to uphold in love, to laugh together, to cry together. But if the crying is not "together" but the result of partner-inflicted blows, the marriage can be said to have already ended. If the laughter is not out of shared joy, but is mocking or derisive put-down, it is not the laughter intended in the vows. "Making cry" and "laughing at" have desecrated them. A groom's vow, undoubtedly genuine in *intent*, is abandoned when *dis*honouring mangles a marriage.

If the vows are broken by the breaking of an arm or a heart, what then? In this scenario there is a clear case for divorce. Why, then, do some women stay?

This was the subject of a university course paper written by Jeanette, a woman I knew some years ago. It was not an academic issue for her, however; not long afterward she made her own decision to leave her extremely abusive husband, taking her two small children with her.

The first point she makes is that the question itself — "Why doesn't she just leave?" — is ill-conceived, or, simply put, a "dumb question." If one tries to give answers that take the question seriously, they will be equally illogical. The question, by its very nature, implies that "she could have left" — that a woman in an abusive marital relationship could, by an act of free will, simply step out of it.

Theoretically, leaving is possible. In fact, leaving an abusive marriage requires an effort of will and a combination of circumstances which stack the odds mightily in favour of "staying." Those who have some practical understanding of the woman abuse scene — victims or shelter workers — know *why* a woman will be beaten, on average, thirty-five times before she leaves her home.

Home. That one word resonates with the germ of an answer. Whatever the number or severity of instances of mental torture, battering, or coerced sexual intimacy, they occurred at home. Home is a wrap-around word, not simply a description of where one happens to live for a year or two or twenty. You woke up at night to attend a sick child — at home. Your kids opened gifts under the Christmas tree — at home. The memories, and even the ongoing experience of tender words and quiet times with a husband who has developed abusive patterns, are about what happened in this livingroom, this bedroom, this kitchen. Your husband gave you flowers that were placed in the vase on that table; it doesn't matter that they are less frequent now and often the day after a beating. A wife and mother who has been abused might say, "This is home, and these are my children. How can I leave?"

To quote from Jeanette's paper:

> ...in expecting a battered woman to quit her rightful domicile, we not only participate in her further victimization but we create further victims; ... To [force her children] to flee with her, or to inflict upon both parties the loss of their symbiotic relation through separation ... provides a powerful reinforcement of criminal behaviour. A batterer is not punished by being made homeless, but his victims are.[3]

I still love the guy!

Sheila is one woman who decided to stay. Late one night, after the children were in bed, she got into a skirmish with her husband, Sam, in the kitchen. It was not unusual for them to push each other around during an argument, having grown up in homes where they both saw their parents shove each other regularly. They both even recalled cheering one or the other parent on.

Sam had been rough before in such tussles. But this time he was drunker than usual. It scared her when he twisted her arm behind her back. She heard it crack. It was broken.

Sheila phoned the police and, by the time the two cruisers arrived, Sam was flat out on the couch, asleep. Sheila also phoned her mother who lived nearby. She arrived just before the police to look after the children, who by now were awake and screaming. One car rushed Sheila to the Emergency Ward of the local hospital. The other took Sam to the station and booked him. In court he pleaded guilty to assault causing bodily harm, and was given sixty days plus six months probation. Sam made good money as a mechanic, and his employer agreed to a "compassionate" leave of absence.

I met Sheila a year after Sam's release. He had quit drinking. He hadn't touched her again, and had taken to heart the judge's warning that a return to court would land him in prison for a lot longer than sixty days.

Sheila and her children attended the church I was serving at the time, and was one of the first women I had talked with directly about a violent home scene. My first question was, "Why did you stay?" She answered, "Better the devil you know than the one you don't."

"I don't get it," I replied naively. She continued, "Can you imagine what it would be like out there if I left? I make peanuts in my job, and Sam's cheque is paying the mortgage, and we're even putting some away. I'd go squirrelly in two days living with my mum, and besides, Sam has always been good about taking the kids to hockey and music. He is still ornery, but he knows I'll be ready for him if he ever lays a hand on me again. I'd get him drunk and kill him. He knows it.

"So that's why I'd rather stay. He thinks I come to church to a Bible Study. If he knew I was in a women's support group, he'd have a bird.... There's another reason. I still love the guy!"

Years later, Sheila and Sam are still together. Sheila continued to live with her fear; what would Sam do if he found out the "Bible Study" was a support group? Sam did not seriously examine his attitudes or behaviour after the slap-on-the-wrist jail term. Their relationship is partly grounded on mutual intimidation, and their now-teenaged children continue to live with the question, "Will it happen again?"

This is not an ideal situation but Sheila and Sam have arrived at a *modus vivendi.* No counsellor, no shelter worker, and no friend has the right to tell Sheila, "You shouldn't have stayed." It is important that women like Sheila be encouraged to stay in touch with support networks and to keep the "flight" option open. They must know that we are cheering them on in their "all things considered" decision. To honour their decisions to "stay," we are wise to pay heed to the observation of the historian, Roderick Phillips:

> In the final analysis we must accept that marriage breakdown is as much a matter of individual as of social definition, and that if a couple in their own personal and social context, were able to integrate a degree of violence into their conceptions of an acceptable and functioning marriage, it would be arrogant of historians to contradict them.[4]

The other side of this story is that Sheila's self-esteem and sense of dignity are intact. She is more aware of her own value as a result of having been in a women's group. She lives her life "around" Sam rather than "with" him; about the only thing they do together are weekend excursions with their children. My guess is that she will leave her hollow marriage down the road, but on her own terms and on her own timetable.

To make you behave

I had been minister of the congregation for four months, and had indicated that family violence was an area of special interest. In preaching and in conversation I had also expressed the view that there are legitimate reasons for leaving an abusive marriage.

After the service one Sunday morning Grace asked to speak with me; it was clearly an urgent matter, and we left the coffee hour at once. "It's about my neighbour," she said, "not me."

"Kathleen is seventy-two, and came to my place for coffee yesterday morning. She and her husband Ross — about seventy-eight, I'd guess — always keep to themselves, so I was surprised when she phoned and asked if she could come over. As soon as she walked into my kitchen, she collapsed into a chair, sobbing. My husband, Don, saw that this was a good time to go out and putter in the yard.

"It was a full five minutes before Kathleen could speak. When she had composed herself, she apologized for taking up my time on a Saturday morning, and had to be convinced that it was okay. She lowered her voice, and asked me never to tell Ross that she had come to see me. He had begun to get cross with her constantly about fifteen years before, and shortly afterwards had started to order her around. Then a few months ago, a new behaviour: if she was too tardy in completing a chore, he would march her to the bathroom and hold her head under the running tap until she promised to do better.

"Then, last week, he ordered her to fill the tub, then held her head under the water as it rose. When he released her, he said it was to make her behave, to teach her a lesson. She had to promise to obey his every command promptly, or else. 'Next time I won't be so easy on you', he'd warned."

I was overwhelmed as Grace unravelled Kathleen's story of marital torture. There were no words; we communicated with our tears. After a moment, she said, "Beatrice wants to talk with you. Would you?"

"Grace, how can I possibly help? Why hasn't she left?"

"Please talk to her; she'll tell you. Ross will be away on Tuesday and Wednesday, and she said she'd call me as soon as he leaves. Could you come to meet her at my place Tuesday morning? I'll call you here at the church." Tuesday morning she called, and fifteen minutes later we were in her livingroom. "How much do you know?" Kathleen asked. I replied, "That your husband holds your head under the water."

Sensing already that the "dumb question" was on the tip of my tongue, she said, "I can't leave. I can't. I'd die before I'd let my children and grandchildren know what's been happening between us. They adore him. They've never seen this side of him, and just wouldn't believe it if I told them why I was leaving. Besides, in my church, saying you'll stay together 'for better, for worse' means always. They don't allow divorce. Besides, lots of women put up with more than being scared once in a while. He'd never drown me; he'd always let my head come up."

"Would you speak with someone from the local women's shelter?" I asked, anticipating a "No" answer.

"Yes!" she exclaimed. Despite her verbal objections to leaving, telling Grace and me was actually the first step of an escape plan.

She was ready to make her move. The next day a staff member from the local women's shelter met Kathleen at Grace's home. Before Ross had returned from his trip that evening she had moved to the shelter. After a separation period they divorced.

And the children and grandchildren? What did they think of Grandma's decision? They had sensed "dark vibes" between Kathleen and Ross for years, and fully supported her decision.

It's your duty

I was having a coffee in Tim Horton's one morning, and was thumbing through a book I had just purchased at the University bookstore — *Abuse and Religion.* Its section headings were blunt, and I was getting deeply immersed in Chapter Six, "Marital Rape." A woman sitting at the next small table had to repeat her question twice to get my attention: "Odd title; what's the book about?"

I was about to mutter an "I-don't-feel-like-talking" response, then realized that her curiosity was earnest, not idle. "About how the church has not been very helpful to victims of family violence," I replied. Her eyes bored into mine.

"Oh," was all she said. She looked at her watch, began to get up from her chair, then sat down again. "I really shouldn't talk to you; I don't even know you." But she went on. "I'm a nurse, and personal stuff is supposed to stay at home. But I'd like to ask you something. I'll bet you're a priest."

"Kind of; a minister."

"Thought so. I haven't gone to church for years — not since I was a kid. We lived in Dublin. My mother — her name is Beth — went to talk to the priest about what my dad, Patrick, was like. He was a monster. He was always hitting Mom or us kids. His temper was so vicious that he would punch walls and kick chairs around. Sober or not, he would smack Mom, but it was worse when he'd been drinking. I was the oldest in the family, and I guess I was about fourteen when Mom asked me to go to see the Father with her. She told him what Dad was like, and that she was thinking seriously about leaving him. Did he have any advice about what she should do? And do you know what he told her?" By now her voice was trembling with anger.

"Tell me," I said.

"He said it was her duty to stay. My God, her *duty*. We went home. Mom took his words as gospel, and never mentioned it to anybody else. She used to be in church every Sunday, but soon we quit going — everybody except Dad. I've never been back, and doubt that I ever will."

Catching herself, she blurted, "Why am I telling you all this? Don't take it personally, Reverend, but what kind of duty is it that could get a person killed?"

"He was wrong to say that," I answered. "Not many clergy would handle it that way nowadays. I hope you give your church another chance."

"Gotta run. Don't dare tell anybody I told you this. By the way, Dad's now old and frail, and Mum is still there. He hasn't hit her in years. I pity him, but I sure don't love him. I just hope he dies before Mum. None of the rest of us would want him."

Safe Havens

My head says, "Recognize Sheila's right to continue living at home with Sam, and the nurse's mother's right to stay with and now to look after a monstrously abusive man." My heart says, "Encourage them to flee while they still can." Because so much of my ministry over the past ten years has been with women and (now grown) children hurt in their own homes, I have developed this view: shut down the abuse as soon as possible and remove the abuser. This applies whether it is abuse during courtship or within a marriage — of one or fifty years.

But this is an ambiguous world. There are few black-and-white certainties. Rather, lots of greys. In particular, as I mentioned earlier, "home" is not merely a place one leaves but a constellation of memories, feelings, and hopes.

There is one source of wisdom, however, that has become integral to the burning question: when does an abused woman take on the wings of a dove, and fly away? I speak of the women's shelters across the land. (See Appendix V for information on contacting shelters.) Many of the women who staff those shelters have experienced marital abuse themselves. The following story suggests a model for cooperation *en route* to community zero tolerance of woman abuse in a linkage between a women's shelter and a hospital.

Jane is a friend of mine and Head Nurse of the Obstetrics unit in a large hospital. She told me of the following cooperative action. For some time a number of women entering the hospital to deliver a baby had either "let it slip" or told an attending nurse directly that she had been punched by her husband during the pregnancy. Some women made light of the incident and added something like, "Its a good thing I'm tough."

After a period of time, the subject was raised at a staff meeting. What, if anything, should be done? A decision was made to raise the question informally with all women who had been admitted: "During your pregnancy did your partner ever hit you?" Now that women had an opportunity to disclose physical abuse as part of an unofficial nursing procedure, the percentage of patients who said "Yes" rose sharply.

An ongoing discussion is being held with the hospital administration as to whether an official protocol can be put in place in which all female patients being admitted to maternity are asked the question upon admission

Since admission nurses currently have no authority to pursue the issue if an abuse disclosure is made, the question of "the next step" was asked. After consultation with the staff of a women's shelter, the following minimum response decision was made. Brochures outlining the programmes of all the shelters in the area would be placed in specially designed racks in the women's washrooms. Any patient or visitor who wished to follow up could make the appropriate phone call or write to the box number herself.

Within a few days the racks had to be replenished. Ever since then, the empty racks have been refilled regularly.

Chapter 7

Sanctuary

> The LORD is a stronghold for the oppressed,
> a stronghold in times of trouble.
>
> — Psalm 9:9

Some Christian traditions place almost exclusive attention on the New Testament, and relegate the Old Testament to the preparatory role of getting us ready for the real gospel. Such churches are generally turned inward, and believe that "salvation" consists in having your own soul protected for eternity. Virtually no attention is given to the church's role as protector and cohealer of the wounded.

Not so for those churches which have a "whole-Bible" understanding of their nature and mission. Jesus made it clear from the beginning of his ministry that his focus was on the vulnerable of society. When his cousin, John the Baptist, sent envoys to challenge him to declare in no uncertain terms what he was up to, he answered them,

> Go and tell John what you have seen and heard: the blind receive their sight, the lame walk, the lepers are cleansed, the deaf hear, the dead are raised, and the poor have good news preached to them. And blessed is anyone who takes no offense at me.
>
> — Luke 7:22-23

Whether it was children who were being kept at arm's length from him by the disciples (Mark 10:13-14), or a woman "taken in adultery" who was about to be executed by a group of self-righteous men (John 8:3-11), or a "demoniac" man relegated to living among the tombstones (Mark 5:1-20), Jesus cared.[1]

Where truth can be told, safely

In the past, churches have not been kind to victims of family violence, and by remaining silent, they have perpetuated that violence. But many congregations are now establishing specific ministries to help both the victims and the perpetrators of domestic violence. These are not simply policy statements at the upper reaches of denominational church government, but pastoral programmes. Raising awareness is central to such programs. The committees are usually low-key, and their members include concerned women and men who have no personal history of family violence, as well as incest survivors, abused women, and former abusers. The goal is to provide friendship and support in a confidential, warm, and caring atmosphere, while finding out more about family violence and how we can help each other. They say "to all who have ears to hear" that many trusted people are in fact hurting their children and their wives; that victims can deal with their memories and hurt in circles of confidentiality. They make no bones about the bottom line: men who abuse must be made aware that what they are doing is not okay even if twisted interpretations of some biblical passages make it seem okay.

Congregations can play a key role in understanding and preventing abuse within the home. For too long, the church has said, "Don't talk about it." Now many congregations are saying, "Here you can tell the truth, safely."

Both the Bible and church history bear ample testimony to the fact that the community of faith has sometimes provided refuge to those escaping danger. Certainly women at risk in their own homes are "refugees," seeking safety and support during a time of crisis. I am not suggesting the establishing of a church shelter as such. The shelter movement has a life of its own, and there is no necessity for a parallel service. Where no women's shelter exists in a community the church might provide start-up funding and organizational support. Some denominational mission grants have already been used for this purpose, usually on a term basis.

The point is that the church is *called*, I believe, to very deliberate and high priority attention to the undoubted crisis of woman abuse. How individual congregations respond to that call is a matter of context and personal commitment. In a community with a well-established and effective shelter network a congregation might play an awareness-raising role.[2]

The Family Justice Committee of First United Church, Mississauga, Ontario, in its first five years has moved from general awareness-raising into crisis counselling and support. Every Saturday morning, a roster of trained volunteers is at the church to provide coffee and conversation in a confidential atmosphere. Women in the community are made aware — mostly through the grapevine — of this opportunity to unburden. With the efforts of this committee their church has become a listening place.[3]

But whatever unique direction a congregation might take in ministry with abused women, the common element must be close contact with the staff of women's shelters who work on the front lines.

The following indicators of possible woman abuse that can be picked up within church circles — as well as possible responses — appeared in a 1991 Special Edition of the United Church mission magazine, *Mandate*. It is so concise, yet thorough, that I repeat it verbatim.[4] Any one or a combination of the clues may indicate that a woman is being hurt at home. The suggested responses are apt if a woman discloses an abusive situation.

SIGNS AND SYMPTOMS

Patterns of absenteeism — interruption of regular attendance at Sunday worship, choir practice, UCW unit meetings, or other regular church activities.

Change in patterns — not sitting in regular place in church, avoiding friends, not staying for coffee after church, etc.

Sudden change in appearance — radical change in clothing or make-up, either well-kept to slovenly, or conservative to seductive.

Refusing pastoral visits at home.

Break in regular contact — the man speaks for her on the phone, at church, etc.

Unusual response to a request to participate in or assist with functions or activities — may be due to no access to transportation, denial of finances, dignity, medical and dental services, etc.

Unusual appearances at the church — showing up at unusual times. For some battered women, church is one place they are allowed to go.

Physical symptons — new glasses, dental work due to broken teeth, hairstyle covering bruises, obvious bruises and injuries such as burns, broken bones, unusual explanation for changes in appearance and/or injuries.

RESPONSES

Take the victim and her story seriously! Do not minimize the violence or the situation. Believe the story. (Minimizing might sound like this: "Oh well, you've both been under quite a strain lately. Have you thought about a holiday together?")

Remember, violence is not a "marital problem." It is a criminal offence. Your goal is not to preserve the marriage, but to secure the safety and well-being of the victim and her children.

Offer your support without over-protecting. (Your position is always to support her ability to act and make decisions. Give her control whenever possible.)

In all that you say and do, undergird the message that battering is completely unacceptable.

At an appropriate time, with the woman, develop a personal protection plan/action strategy.

In cooperation with the woman make an appropriate referral to local crisis resource centres.

Follow-up: make regular contact with the victim following the disclosure and maintain a supportive friendship.

If the woman goes to a shelter, support her efforts to live a life free from violence. If she returns to the violent male after being in a shelter (or elsewhere) do not be surprised.

***Do* ask her consent** before taking any action. Never discuss the matter with her husband *without* her consent and approval. You could put her at greater risk.

We have been speaking of what a group of people within a congregation can do in response to the need for support ministries for abused women. Now let's look at what ministry *staff* might do, besides supporting such groups.

Some years ago I was on a committee organizing an awareness-raising workshop on family abuse for clergy. The workshop leaders were all in place, and we were meeting with the main presenter. She was a well-known and highly respected counsellor with a local family services agency. Out of the blue, she asked, "Why aren't you inviting church secretaries to the workshop?"

We asked her to explain. She said, "Don't you realize how often a woman will either phone or come by the church to talk with the secretary. Not the minister. The secretary. For one thing, she is likely female, and it is highly unlikely that a woman being hurt at home would speak to a male about her situation — even, especially, a male minister. In fact, chances are that she'll ask the secretary not to tell the minister what she's heard."

We were amazed, and I couldn't wait to get back to the church to ask my secretary about the revelation. She confirmed it. "Yes," she said, "a woman will often come in — just to talk — and before you know it she's talking about some home stuff. And yes, they usually ask me not to mention it to you." What a lesson in anonymous pastoral ministry!

Unless he has given some pretty clear signals from the pulpit or in some other public way that he is interested pastorally in family violence, and is somewhat aware of the issues, a hurting woman will not see a male minister as a possible supportive resource. Even a female minister will be approached for counsel and support only if she has put out the signal loud and clear that she is concerned and willing to spend lots of time in conversation.

How do ministers get the word out that they are interested and aware? When I was deeply immersed in prison ministry some years ago I was invited by the Elizabeth Fry Society of Hamilton to speak with volunteers and staff about the impact of child sexual assault on female offenders. The claim that virtually all of the inmates at the Kingston Prison for Women (P4W) had been victims of incest was being discussed, and women in the group who were very familiar with P4W were confirming that statistic.

Curious, I asked this question: "How many of you have ever heard a sermon on incest?" Not a hand went up, my own included. In a group of twenty-two or so women, not one had heard incest dealt with from the pulpit. And of all the "social issue" themes I had tried to address in sermons in thirty years of preaching, not once had I mentioned incest. When I confessed this, one woman asked pointedly, "What did your silence *say* to women or to girls who were victims of incest?" She answered her own question: "That there was nothing wrong with it, especially since the trusted adult perpetrator had likely tried to convince her that it was okay."

A month later I had occasion to supply-preach at a local church. I wasn't using the common lectionary at the time; sadly, none of the ecumenical readings ever deal with family violence, even though the Bible does. (See Appendix VI for an exploration of these texts.) My text was Amnon's incestuous rape of his half-sister Tamar (II Samuel 13). At the end I added a line that was not in my script, "If any of you fathers are committing incest against your daughters, please stop!" Two men whispered "Thank you" to me at the door as they shook my hand firmly. I think I can read eyes well enough to know what they meant.

Unless a minister says something publicly about the evil of family violence, it is unlikely that someone being hurt will see the minister as a resource. Unless an abused woman hears it said loud and clear from the pulpit that the preacher is aware of the problem and would try to help, she *might* unload her pained burden on the church secretary, but with the rider, "Please don't tell the minister."

There is a parallel lesson to be learned from the field of medicine. Dr. David Gordon White had received some posters and buttons from The Women's Directorate of Ontario which read, "There's No Excuse for Wife Assault. It is a Crime." He chose not to display the posters or to wear a button because he didn't think a medical office should be politicized. But his office secretary did wear one, and told Dr. White that some unnamed long-time patients had disclosed to her that they been assaulted by their husbands over the years. None of his patients had ever spoken of abuse to him so he decided to wear a button. Sure enough, with the button as an ice-breaker, some patients who had been coming to him for years did disclose serious marital abuse. He writes, "Wearing this small piece of plastic provided me with more concrete results than anything I had read or heard about wife assault, probably because it made communication much easier."[5]

He had broken the silence. So can the church. And to replace the silence there can be gospel words of healing support for those who wear bruises under their Sunday best.

The "I care" pulpit

The minister can play a key role in the establishing of a "safe place" congregation. The church as sanctuary. By the law of the mediaeval church, a fugitive from justice, or a debtor, was immune from arrest so long as he was in a "holy place" (sanctus means "holy"). The term is now used to mean any place where a person might be safe from harm. There are many things that a minister can do either in support of a specific sanctuary strategy, or, where there is none, to make a personal statement of support, starting from the pulpit.

The Common Lectionary is in general use among clergy, but one would have to go outside it in order to locate a biblical context/text for preaching on family violence. There are many such biblical texts, but only a genuine sense of call, a "beckoning from the text," would motivate the preacher to want to identify and exegete them. One could start with the best known family violence texts — Cain and Abel (Genesis 4:1-16), the incestuous rape of Tamar (II Samuel 13:1-11), the violation of trust lament (Psalm 55) and the notorious subjugation passages (Genesis 3:16, Ephesians 5:22-24). It would take nerve to challenge the "husband-as-head" mind-set which is so predominant in scripture, but unless the preacher takes on and contextualizes such biblical passages, she or he need not expect any pastoral requests from hurting wives or abusing partners.

A "Darkside Lectionary," called "Reality, with Hope" is found in Appendix VI. It draws attention to the many appropriate violence-against-women texts which could be used homiletically in a modern setting. A minister who feels drawn to family violence preaching could, with the help of a concordance, explore those passages in which women are hurt by men. There are also marvellous mending-side stories. It is only by trying to get inside the stories that you will be able to communicate what the Bible does say about violence and abuse and what lessons we can learn from it today.

Worship services and discussion groups

Congregations that already have a Family Justice Committee, or something comparable, are well equipped to conduct a special worship service. The committee could lead a service in their home congregation and visit others. One congregation recently held a covenanting service to honour the special call to ministry in family violence. Be ready, however, for the response which one such touring troupe got at the door after the service: "That's all fine and dandy, but why talk about that abuse stuff in a church?" It came as a surprise to me initially to learn that the percentage of women who are being abused or have been abused is the same in congregations as in the community — twenty-nine percent. With three exceptions, every scenario described in this book involves a church family. Congregations are no more free from woman abuse than the rest of the population.

Other ways to encourage discussion of woman abuse in the congregation include after service forums and special "outreach" evenings. Shelter staff are more than willing to explain ways in which congregations might be supportive of people being hurt at home. The Elizabeth Fry Society works with women who have horrendous histories of child and adulthood abuse; their staff would also welcome the opportunity to speak to a congregation.

If family abuse issues are raised in Sunday morning worship or in church discussion groups it is likely that one in four women present has experienced emotional abuse, and that one in ten has experienced physical abuse. If a woman's husband has insisted on sexual intimacy without her consent, then she will tune in at once to the message that intimacy which is *not* mutual is rape.[6]

The point is not to expect or elicit disclosure in some immediate way; that would be a macabre and cruel. There might possibly be times when a woman will want to speak to a friendly listener soon after the service or discussion. But normally someone who identifies abuse against herself and the opportunity for mending will choose her first confidant very cautiously, and it is not likely to be a minister. If the long-term pulpit message is an unmistakable sensitivity to family hurt with the underlying invitation to mending-directed disclosure, then a woman may be encouraged to reach out to the church for help.

But how should the church or the minister respond to such disclosure? It would be pointless to try to provide a complete "how to" guide for response. Each situation is different, and defies a pat "solution." But here are some of practical starters — "dos" and "don'ts" — which may help to prepare the ground for churches that want to be equipped to counsel in depth in a disclosure situation:

DO

Do listen. Resist any temptation to tell other abuse stories in a misguided attempt to show your empathy.

Do read the current literature. Appendix II lists some titles for anyone who wants to go below the surface.

Do interpret abuse passages in the Bible. Familiarize yourself with some significant biblical accounts of family abuse, and thereby be in a position to relate "spirit" to "reality."

Do preach about dysfunctional family life. When you do, publicize it well in the local media; there might well be people with little previous church affiliation who would want to hear a church or synagogue perspective.

Do develop worship resources. Women's and men's groups, as well as committees in the congregation, would appreciate suggestions on how the theme of ministry with abused partners might be wrapped into worship opportunities.

Do alert the wider church. Use your influence to encourage an emphasis on such ministry in wider church workshops, gatherings, conferences, etc.

Do know the law. Perhaps with the assistance of a lawyer find out what the Criminal Code says about family violence, including the range of punitive sanctions available to the judiciary. Be ready to acknowledge that such sanctions (including a prison sentence) might be necessary and appropriate in a given situation.

Do network. Know the names of other aware clergy in the community (of whatever denomination or faith tradition), and be ready to *refer* an abused person to someone with more experience or skills. (You'll be called on too as you develop awareness, competence, and confidence.)

Do connect with a women's shelter. If it is a case of physical abuse, do not hesitate to recommend leaving the violent situation, maybe the same day. Be ready with information about local shelters.

Do invite community resource people. One of the best ways to raise awareness in the congregation is to arrange after-church forums, etc., for informal sharing around abuse issues. This also lets agencies and shelters in your community know of those clergy and congregations that *they* can call upon.

DON'T

Don't try to mediate. Classical models of marriage counselling, i.e., both partners always being present, are entirely inappropriate. Recall the pervasive control/power tactic used by all abusers (Chapter 1).

Don't give advice. But be ready with suggestions for helpful reading or human resources in the community (e.g., a shelter counsellor).

Don't counsel both partners. If both partners wish to have counselling, "network." Professional agency people should normally be called in to help, or, if you and other clergy in the community have developed some skills in marital abuse counselling, female clergy might counsel the woman and a male clergy the husband. (Obviously there would be exceptions.)

Don't be naive. Be aware of such potentially dangerous side-effects of woman abuse as stalking, murder, and suicide (by either partner).

Don't give up. If you start to take an interest in marital violence ministry and find it overwhelming, persist anyway. Continue to let it be known that you care deeply about people hurt within marriage.

These suggestions provide only a starting point. The best way to canvass ways in which a congregation and its clergy might play an active role in family abuse ministry would be for interested people to "brain-storm" around both the need and the possibilities. The study suggestions at the end of this book (Appendix I) offer some ideas about how men's or women's groups might discuss the issues in depth. The challenge to respond to woman abuse cannot be ignored or forever put on the back burner. Churches must take up the challenge as part of a ministry of healing.

No longer a punching bag

When one congregation moved family abuse ministry up to the front burner, the impact was profound. Karen was raised in a European country where the violence just wouldn't go away after the armistice agreements ending World War II had been signed. Many homes from which young men strode proudly to war remained sullen in defeat. Soldiers returned home, not to victory parades on the main street, but to silence. Many asked themselves, ruefully, "Why did we fight?" For some, an unconquered violence lay coiled within, waiting for a victim. Anger that the victorious armies smothered in occupation seethed beneath the surface.

One such returned soldier was John, who married Karen in a post-war wedding. He was twenty-two, Karen was seventeen. Early days at home were light, and Karen was ecstatically happy that she was so quickly developing the cooking and housekeeping skills that John at first hoped, then *demanded* that she perfect. Karen didn't mind. And their decision after two years of marriage to emigrate to Canada overwhelmed her with a joy which drowned out his shouting and steady carping. She knew that a steady anger was starting to take shape inside her as well, but she dare not let it out. Besides, after they were settled in a new country they would both simmer down, raise children, and get away from the chaos.

They moved to the Maritimes but the "geographical cure" did not work. John's shouting became punching, daily, and Karen's defence was literally to soften the blows by gaining weight. Within two years she was obese. She described it later as making herself into a human punching bag. When they had a son Karen recalls thinking, "Oh no, not another John!"

I met Karen at a congregation-sponsored event on family violence. She had left John many years before when his violence became life-threatening, and had raised her son in a small, southern Ontario town. We sat at the same table, and over coffee she told me her story. She said that when she had seen the poster advertising the event, called "Coping: Your Church Can Help," she couldn't believe her eyes. The church? How could it possibly help her to deal with the hurt, anger, and suicidal despair which had tumbled around inside her for decades? And how could it possibly help her to deal with her multiple personality disorder? She had been in therapy on more than one occasion, but there always seemed to be a piece missing. As a woman of deep faith, she kept asking, "How could God just stand there and let it happen, and why does Jesus think I should forgive that cruel man?" Therapy, although helpful, had never probed the spiritual depth required to deal with these questions.

She had never before attended a United Church service, and she had doubts as she entered the sanctuary the next morning to worship. The service was on the theme of God's healing power for those hurt at home. The sermon, based on the story in Mark, Chapter 5, about Legion, dealt with the healing ministry of Jesus with a man who was demon-possessed and self-lacerating — a man with a multiple personality disorder! The message was that there can be healing in our day for those who have been so hurt that they "become" many people in order to disassociate from that one (now among many) whose dignity was being destroyed and that self-laceration is a common, if misguided, attempt to smother emotional pain.

Karen said to me some weeks later that the church had provided a ministry that weekend that she had been aching for. She kept attending, took membership classes, joined the congregation, and later helped to organize an abused women's support group. She is gradually losing the enormous amount of weight she had put on. Is she a survivor? "No," she says happily, "I'm a thriver. When I discovered that Jesus heard a broken-up man crying in a cemetery, I knew he'd hear me too."

Can the church help? In more ways than one. Think, pray — and act! Many women and men in the congregation will be glad you did. Be a sanctuary. Be a place where "Cry" can be safely screamed and where "Response" will be immediate, tough, and informed.

Chapter 8

Break the Silence

> Nothing is covered up that will not be uncovered, and nothing secret that will not become known. Therefore whatever you have said in the dark will be heard in the light, and what you have whispered behind closed doors will be proclaimed from the housetops.
>
> — LUKE 12:2-3

They stood at a distance, saying nothing. The absence of the disciples was a deafening roar of abandonment. His mother, his aunt, Salome, and "the beloved disciple" were there (Matthew 27:55f). But the silence of the others said loud and clear, "We won't get involved," and was surely as heart-breaking as Peter's betrayal, "I do not know him."

History is full of the betrayal of bystanders in the face of grievous wrong. As Jews were being rounded up in Nazi Germany, the Dietrich Bonhoeffers who spoke out were the exception, not the rule. The Vatican knew what was happening. Protestant church leaders knew. But most were silent.

When Japanese-Canadians in British Columbia were branded as "enemy aliens" during World War II and were being herded onto trains for destinations unknown, few church representatives protested. Even when the war had ended the official church voices were largely silent — although the Student Christian Movement spoke out — in demanding the return of confiscated property and encouraging that the dislocated families be allowed to return home.

These and countless other events in history reveal that despite high-flown faith statements and mission action plans, the church has not been among the first to raise its voice in outrage at abuses and violations against the vulnerable. There seems to be a built-in "wait-and-see" attitude when abuse and violence surface, a false hope that things will get better on their own.

In the case of violence against women, Carleton University historian Roderick Phillips outlines some of the most patent examples of the church's arm's length attitude toward woman abuse in his book *Untying The Knot* (See Appendix IV). From active encouragement of a degree of "disciplining" of one's wife, through a gradual acknowledgment that anything more than "moderate" disciplining might be wrong, to today's still muted objection to woman beating, the church, by and large, has not been an advocate for change. It has not "spoken out on behalf of" (*ad-vocare*) women who are hurt at home.

I Herrens Vold

In 1985 I was in Norway studying that country's criminal justice system. On a train between Bergen and Oslo I happened to meet Eva Lundgren, then a member of the Faculty of Religious Studies at the University of Bergen (now in the Department of Sociology of The University of Uppsala, Sweden). Her field was Church and Society; it did not take long to identify our common interest in studying the church's ministry with victims of domestic violence. She had just written a book called *I Herrens Vold* (in English *In the Grip of the Lord*). The cover of the book portrays a cross superimposed over an image of a husband beating his wife on their bed.

Eva's English was far better than my halting Norwegian, and she told me — with many conversational silences — about the subject matter of the book. The silences were not all because she was searching for an appropriate English word. Most of them were because of the dreadful content of the book. I could hardly believe what I was hearing.

I Herrens Vold is about woman abuse within the Christian community. The ten wives who were interviewed for the book thought that they *deserved* the beatings. They and their husbands were members of a charismatic revival movement which had been introduced to Norway from the United States in 1970. It had grown quickly and, at the time of Eva's interviews, some 200 revivalist groups were spread across the country. They first drew media attention because they were practising ritual exorcism of demons that supposedly possessed the women. Only the women.

Lundgren's research had unearthed the startling fact that in those revivalist circles, not only had the women been persuaded that they were demon-possessed, but had been made to believe that because they were so evil their husbands' assaults were not "abuse" but "discipline." Helene, one of the ten women interviewed for the book, said the following in a broadcast interview on Norwegian Radio:

> [My husband, Mikael] has to — he has to hit, hit me — once in awhile. For example, I resist if ...if I am supposed to sew something, I just don't want to sew and he has to force me to do it. I have to do it to fulfill my duty as a woman. But, but, it's just showing that he really cares about me. He cares about guiding me onto the right path. So that's why ... why I understand that it's, it's, it's love, genuine love on his part. And it costs him a great deal — because hitting someone he loves causes him to suffer. But he has to do it because he takes the place of Christ — where I am concerned. He is my Lord, and Christ disciplines him and he disciplines me. That is the way of Christianity. So I feel that ... although it hurts physically, I can understand that it is .... Once in a while I can't understand it, and then I get angry and confused and sad. But when I think about it afterwards I realize that it is right. Because it is the path to God.[1]

Professor Lundgren then described for me the incredible pain she felt as she heard the women's stories — each one a pitiful defence of their husbands' abuse, and each one couched in the language of faith. During the interviews she found herself moving away from the "proper" objective stance of a social scientist. Anger was building up in her towards the husbands who had so cruelly mistreated their wives, but even more so towards the fundamentalist revivalism that sanctioned woman abuse in the name of "the Lord."

My conversation with Eva Lundgren and subsequent reading of her work stirred within me an uncanny and even shameful realization: my liberal "tolerance" of certain traditions of faith and practice within Christianity was aiding and abetting woman abuse. The fact that I had been ignorant of such stark abuse before meeting Eva gave me small comfort. Now I knew, and what would I do?

Certainly I could no longer remain silent. In those situations where a faith tradition endorses and even encourages what is plainly a criminal act, soft ecumenism cannot be invoked as an excuse for silence and inaction. The atrocities committed in the name of Jesus by the Children of God and other mind-binding sects are a case in point: we do not turn a blind eye to their criminality because they are "fellow Christians." Rather we unhesitatingly name the crime, and reject their practices along with their bogus doctrines.

But how does the Norwegian research of Eva Lundgren and her colleagues impact on *us*? What evidence is there that the same phenomenon happens in Canada? In fact, some Christian denominations in Canada do actively encourage husbands to "discipline" their wives — physically, if necessary — and they support the practice with biblical warrant:

> Wives, in the same way [that Jesus accepted his abuse], accept the authority of your husbands, so that, even if some of them do not obey the word, they may be won over without a word by their wives' conduct, when they see the purity and reverence of your lives. (1 Peter 3:1-2)

I Peter 3:1-2 you know

In pre-marriage counselling I still meet couples of whom at least one has been raised in a church environment that condones a husband's disciplining of his wife by physical punishment, often spanking. Five years ago I was told by Martha, a member of a victims' advocacy group of which I was a member, that in her denomination the husband was unequivocally the head of the household, which entitles him to strike his wife if he thought it necessary to teach her a lesson. I could hardly believe my ears.

"Today," I gasped, "today in your church that is condoned?"

"Yes," she replied, "not only condoned, but *taught* as an article of marriage morality. I Peter 3:1-2, you know."

That's actually what Martha said to me in defense of a practice she had seen and grown up with. In her home it had not been at all uncommon for her mother to be berated and disciplined by her father. She recalled vividly how her father would first give a lecture to the children about the Lord's will and his own responsibility for the management of the home — as head. Then he would strike his wife in plain view of the children. Martha also knew that at her denomination's local theological college the husband's headship of the home, including his responsibility for disciplining his children and his wife, was taught in the course in Christian ethics.

And a time to bolt

Not many months after Martha had told me this story I had occasion to be counselling a young couple for marriage. When Jen, the bride-to-be told me her denomination, I did a double take. It was the same as Martha's — and her family were members of the same congregation. Neither Jen nor the groom, Jacques, was United Church, and when I asked why they wanted me to marry them, she said that because Jacques was "not saved" (read, not of their conservative persuasion), he would not be welcome in their home or their church. She had "bolted," said she was going to marry him anyway, and defied her father's "order" to quit seeing him. Until a few days before the wedding Jen did not know if her family would attend. After saying they would not, they relented and came.

At the rehearsal her father was incredibly rude and, as he walked with his daughter down the aisle, his face was a portrait of rage. Jen had told me in the counselling sessions that her father frequently scolded her mother, and had on occasion "disciplined" her physically.

This husband-wife dynamic happens in *our* communities. I have not yet had the temerity to speak publicly about that denomination's Christian family ethic. Saying it here moves me closer to breaking that silence. But what can we do? In our neighbourhoods, at bridge gatherings, in letters to the editor, we can say loudly and clearly that woman abuse is wrong.[2] There has to be some way in which women, who are caught within situations where abuse is sanctioned by their churches and their families, can hear the other side.

My own pre-marriage counselling style and agenda have changed greatly since I have become more informed about abuse at home. Since so many home scenes are hurtful, it *has* to be assumed that some of the couples that clergy marry will become abusive; in such cases, chances are that abuse has already begun.

Make-up covered the bride's scratches

When Chester and his best man came into the vestry before the wedding ceremony on that gorgeous Saturday, I was startled by the red bruises on his cheeks. He noted my surprise, and explained with his head down: "Wait 'till you see Vera's face. Umm, we had a fight after the rehearsal party last night. We knew we shouldn't have taken that first beer, but we did. Before you know it we had taken three, four. I gave her a blast about something stupid; I don't even remember what it was. She swore at me, and I shoved her. She clawed my face — as you can see. My God, Mort, I don't know what happened."

I was overcome with shock and sadness. I had gotten to know Vera and Chester over a period of years. She had been knocked around and, on one occasion, hospitalized by her first husband. I had met her through my work with a community women's shelter. I met Chester when I was a volunteer with a local John Howard Society branch. He was on parole, having served prison time for crimes involving violence, and we struck up a coffee-shop friendship.

Chester and Vera met at a meeting of AA. They fell in love immediately, and after a few weeks of "we're in heaven" glee, they asked if I would marry them. They had been looking for just such a mate all their lives, and they just *knew* that they were meant for each other. I ought to have been wary in a supportive kind of way, but instead I responded with great enthusiasm. I knew them so well that I decided to meet them only twice instead of my normal four interviews. They held hands during both sessions, and mooned over one another in what I thought was a beautiful new love of a kind neither had ever known.

They were both problem drinkers, and had both toyed with the "idea" of AA long before joining. So when they met there it seemed to them both that they would be mutually supportive. I knew that they were "sipping" in the last weeks before the wedding, but did not question their motives: this was a celebration time, after all, and after they were married, they'd get back into the AA program.

I couldn't have been more naive. My casual acquiescence to their "just for now" return to alcohol was, as I look back, totally unhelpful. After all, I had moved in AA circles for long enough to know that "just this once" is the push down the slippery slope.

Back to the wedding ceremony. The male wedding party stood at the front of the church, the bridal processional started, and my knees turned to water when I saw Vera walking toward me. She was crying. The make-up which had been larded over the welts on her face was running under her anguished tears. Moments later a life-long marriage was being promised that I feared would not last a year. Believing that, I still asked them to say their vows, wondering if a miracle might help them stay together.

There was no miracle. The reception was an embarrassing drinking party. Vera and Chester ended their marriage four months later.

Not long afterward I moved and lost touch with those two lost souls for whom breaking silence about what was happening between them might have led to an authentic relationship. A "tough love" pastoral approach with them might have involved my canceling the ceremony. So what if the church was full of wedding guests? So what if I might have been accused of being blatantly patronizing? Was my silence in the face of a situation crying out for response and mending real ministry?

You decide. I have replayed that marriage ceremony tape over and over in my mind many times, and still do not know exactly where I should have stepped in. If ministers are responsible for marrying couples do they not also shoulder some responsibility for what happens after the wedding? The Book of Ecclesiastes speaks of "a time to keep silence, and a time to speak" (3:7b). The trick is to know what time it is.

In our everyday circles there are signs of hurting which we generally ignore out of the old adage that what people do at home is their own business. Maybe we should re-think that. Do some of the "times to speak" include times when co-workers, friends, or family are hurting or being hurt?

I recall so vividly my conversations with Eva Lundgren, and the commitment I made to her then to speak out where possible. The two main "platforms" I have had are pulpit and the written page. Breaking the silence also takes many other forms. If you are being hurt at home, tell someone. If your neighbour is being hurt, tell someone. Let no one be in doubt about where *you* stand. Wherever possible invite shelter workers to speak at meetings and from the pulpit in your church.[3]

Unless men challenge other men eyeball-to-eyeball, abusers will continue to believe that zero tolerance doesn't include them. One way in which men are trying to do just that is by marching in solidarity with women who have been hurt. "Men Walking Against Male Violence Against Women" has become a very visible expression of that solidarity. Walk, wear a white ribbon, do something that will signal to the women you know, and to your children, that you are speaking out.[4] Unless all of us — women and men together — work against woman abuse in whatever ways we can, then we will not be part of the solution; our silence will still be part of the problem.

PART III

MENDING

When the woman saw that she could not remain hidden, she came trembling; and falling down before him, she declared in the presence of all the people why she had touched him, and how she had been immediately healed. He said to her, "Daughter, your faith has made you well; go in peace."

— LUKE 8:47-48

Chapter 9

Dignity Restored

O LORD my God, I cried to you for help,
and you have healed me ...
Weeping may linger for the night,
but joy comes with the morning.

— PSALM 30:2,5B

One of my daughters read a few pages into the second draft of this book, then put it aside. "Dad, its so sad," she said, "I can't read any more of it right now. How were you able to write it?" Indeed, "Cry" is a sad tale. My suggestions for what can be done in "Response" seem so pitifully inadequate. And my eyes were moist as I put to paper many of the stories, for voices cracking with hurt kept echoing within me.

I want now to identify rays of hope which shine from the lives of women who have "made it" after being hurt at home. They are a special group of people; they are thrivers. The language of recovery from abuse has moved a lot in the past decade, from "victim," to "survivor," to "thriver." For many years the talk-show craze, for example, has nourished the image of woman-as-victim. Self-identification by one's victimization seemed a necessary qualification for being a guest on the show — even, in some circles, for being a "real woman." In the early years of public disclosure of abuse in the eighties, the slogan seemed to be "I am what was done to me" (victim). Then the slogan became "I am how I made it" (survivor).

To be a thriver is a step further along the road: it is to identify oneself apart from an abuse history. Not that it has been forgotten or ignored. Rather the hurt has been dealt with, usually with a form of forgiveness that we shall discuss below. The slogan could well be, "I am fully dignified woman, by virtue of the strength in me!" This is not to deny that the memories will not resurface from time to time (for example, around anniversary dates). They will need different kinds of attention, but the basic healing has happened, and dignity is intact.

Perhaps, as you read this, you are *still* being hurt at home. If so, don't get down on yourself. Do not think of yourself as *not yet* a survivor, let alone a thriver. You will be. Be gentle with yourself. While the bruises to heart or body are still painful, you can't pull yourself together in a valiant effort of bravery. While the hurting still engulfs you, you are still trying to decide: what shall I do? When the hurt is past, you'll make small steps back into a healthy relationships with friends, family, and possibly even the partner who hurt you.

There is no single recipe for becoming a thriver again, with a renewed sense of dignity. But here are five stories about women who had been badly hurt in their marriages. They show us that the hope for full restoration of dignity is not in vain. These women won. Today they are happy, and have never been more self-assured.

I'm gold!

My first conversation with Teresa occurred many years ago at a United Church General Council meeting in Montreal. We were in the same table group, and during one of the coffee-breaks she poured out to me an admission that the main reason she attended such church meetings was for emotional survival. The home scene was dreadful, an unremitting stream of emotional and verbal abuse. Nothing she did was right. She illustrated her husband Andrew's incessant condemnation by describing her recent attempt to wallpaper the kitchen. Her mother had come over to help, and they both knew they had to "get it right" in order to meet Andrew's high expectation of excellence. Over the eight years of their marriage, Teresa had even bought into his motto: "get it right the first time." In her youth she had often been lackadaisical about the quality of performance, be it at the piano or writing a school essay. To strive for excellence seemed like an improvement in her character. Her mother also applauded Andrew's good influence on Teresa, for she had "improved a lot" since marrying him. Besides, it wasn't a bad idea for their four-year old son Drew to see his parents "go for the gold."

Back to the kitchen. Neither Teresa nor her mother was prepared for the ferocity of Andrew's verbal attack when he scrutinized the results of their wallpapering efforts after coming home from the office. He made a bee-line from the door to the kitchen to inspect. He stood back, murmured approval, then ran his fingers along the creases where strips of wallpaper had been joined together. Beside one cupboard there was a tiny gap, so small you'd have to be looking for it. As he tore the strip from the wall, he snarled, "Can't you *ever* get it right?"

Each such explosion had torn a piece from her heart, and she concluded that Montreal coffee-break conversation by saying, "I deserve better."

When I met Teresa three years later she told me that the marriage had ended not long after her return home from Montreal. In retrospect she realized the impact the music at General Council had had on her. She recalls weeping freely during the hymns, and all week feeling the presence of Jesus, with his quiet and affirming attitude toward women. She had attended her own church for years, and was an active Presbyter. But somehow in those familiar faith-settings she had not been open to receiving the strength to address the slow erosion of her self-esteem. She believes she'd actually been blocking out any voice that said, "You deserve better" for fear that she might do what she'd vowed never to do: leave her marriage. In Montreal that gentle voice kept saying to her, "You deserve better." She was listening, and believing it.

For two years before Teresa's flight from the marriage, she was an emotional wreck. During the separation and subsequent divorce time she'd been supported by her family and church. I remarked that she seemed six inches taller. She replied, "I am — inside, where it counts! And the best thing of all is that Drew's doing fine. He's with me, but he sees his dad every weekend."

"How did you manage to survive and then thrive?" I asked her. Her biggest support had been the church choir. (Andrew used to "joke" to friends that her choir would fit in better beside a lily pond). Since returning from Montreal she'd sing and hum the

Sunday words and music of anthems and hymns for weeks after they'd been used. Her low self-esteem had been rescued before it dropped even further, largely by the constant reassurance of those words. Besides, she was now *hearing* the sermons with their salvation message of restored dignity and grace. What the minister was saying was always uncannily relevant to the particulars of her state of mind at the time. Teresa recalls thinking so often, "She's talking about me; I am right in the middle of that Bible story!"

After the separation she and Drew lived in a very modest apartment until the house had been sold and she was able to live in her own private home again. (The strip off the kitchen wall never did get replaced). For Teresa, living in her own home was an important part of her restoration to a sense of dignity.

Will she marry again? Maybe, she says, but not until she has been a "thriver" long enough to feel "Teresa is a beautiful child of God" on a daily basis. She still has periods when Andrew's "Why can't you ever get it right?" condemnation rings in her ears. But the sense of her own beauty and dignity which had gradually shrivelled under Andrew's constant verbal assaults had never hit rock bottom. And she would never, ever, allow anyone to do that to her again. Yes, she'd like to be with someone, someday. But in the meantime she's delighted to be happy, fulfilled, and a complete person... alone, with her son. Singing in the choir, taking an active part in The United Church Women, and worshipping every Sunday give her about all the joy she can handle right now. Tomorrow? "Well, we'll see," she smiles. "Right now I'm still getting used to being gold!"

There was another dimension of Teresa's journey to thriving I was curious about. So I asked her not long ago, "Have you forgiven Andrew?" A pause.

"Yes. That was the last part of the journey. My mother can't understand why I have, especially since she remembers so vividly his tirade in the kitchen. But for me the bottom line of the gospel is forgiveness, and it has to be part of my new dignity. In The Lord's Prayer we ask God to 'forgive us our trespasses, as we forgive those who trespass against us.' And on the cross Jesus said, 'Father, forgive them; for they know not what they do.' So forgiving Andrew was something I had to do."

I asked if Andrew had ever admitted having hurt her, and Teresa replied that he had not. Initially that had made forgiveness impossible, she said, but she's past that. It's for her own sake that she's forgiven him.

Forgiveness is an important ingredient in the healing journey after wife abuse; some would say the *key* ingredient. The verb "to forgive" is a translation of the Greek verb *aphiemi*. It means literally "to set aside," "to let go," or "to release." To forgive a loan, the image which is prominent in Matthew's version of The Lord's Prayer (6:12), means to release the debtor from the obligation of repayment. The debt has been cancelled, let go. The Greek for Jesus' prayer from the cross is *"Pater, aphes autois, ou gar oidasin ti poiousin"* (23:34), literally, "Father, release them, for they do not know what they are doing." In The Lord's Prayer the Greek text of Luke has *"aphes hemin tas hamartias hemon,"* again literally, "release (set aside) our sins." (11:4).

This does not mean that the sin is *forgotten* or wiped out, as if it had never been. What it does mean is that the one who was hurt is relieved of the burden of having to deal any further with the hurter. The question, "What shall I do about him?" is handed over, as it were, to God. "God, *you* deal with him; I can't, and I won't."[1]

It intrigues me that Jesus asked God to forgive those who were crucifying him; he did not say, "I forgive them." The principle is the same whether it is a request from the cross or from a battered wife: God is invoked as the one who will deal with the hurter.

You Christians preach forgiveness

Some years ago I was confronted by an angry, still hurting, woman in her twenties who had been sexually molested by her father when she was a child. Victoria had agreed with a friend's suggestion that she speak with someone about the rage that was tearing her apart. She and her friend came to my office to talk.

"You Christians preach forgiveness," Victoria began. "Do you have any idea what it is like to remember that your first sexual partner was your dad? I hate him. He destroyed my childhood. He robbed me of the mystery of first intimacy. Every time I relate sexually with my husband, it is my dad's arms, my dad's mouth, my dad's penis that hold, kiss, and come into me. And you expect me to forgive him?"[2]

I made no attempt to defuse her anger. Words would have been cruel. Only silence was appropriate. Then, in a barely audible voice Victoria said, "Help me; God, help me." The words weren't directed to me. They were a prayer.

After a few moments I ventured, "He's still doing it to you."

"Doing what?"

"Molesting you. Your fully justified anger is at the continuation, years later, of his sexual invasion of a little girl. It is a grim afterplay — twenty years later."

She looked at me, her eyes moist, her hands trembling. "How can I stop him?" she pleaded.

"Take the memory," I replied, "take the anger, take the hurt, and put them into a bag. Give the bag to God, and say, 'God, I don't want to deal with this stuff any more. I'm giving it to you — all of it. You'll know what to do. I never have to know — I just trust that you'll do what has to be done'."

Her look was both pained and quizzical. I glanced at her friend, who looked equally puzzled. "Mort, this isn't children's story time," she said. "What are you trying to say?"

I told them that a survivor (now thriver) who led a Mennonite-based women's support group had done just that. She had literally prayed the continuing burden of her father's childhood sexual invasion of her into the hands of God. God relieved her of the burden, and from that moment the albatross of that memory ceased to weigh her down. Yes, she still had flash-backs. Yes, she had a long way to go. But the basic issue had been dealt with. She had released the anger and the pain into God's care — *aphiemi.* She had forgiven him.

"Victoria," I said, "try it. It worked for my Mennonite friend. In the gospel meaning of the word — *aphiemi* — forgive your father."

Her friend called a month later. "She's done it. She prayed her anger into God's hands and she's freed. Wait 'till you see her!"

This is no trick; it is a faith-miracle. A woman of faith can let go of the deep anger which results from the abuse of her husband. Yes, she *can* forgive him and this is crucial to her own restoration of lost dignity; much more important to her than to the abuser.

There are many passages in scripture which reflect healing and "restoration of dignity." The whole tenor of this book has been that the "mending" motif may be understood as the core of the gospel announcement of good news. Reaching out to the hurting was definitely at the top of Jesus' agenda, especially as portrayed by Luke, "the beloved physician" (Luke 7:18-23; see Colossians 4:14).

John's story of Jesus' evident compassion for the woman who was being unjustly killed (8:2-11) may be regarded as a mini-gospel. The graciousness with which he accepted — responded to — the simple affections of Mary (Luke 10:39-42; John 12:3) present a dramatic alternative to the patriarchal power dynamic based on "*I* (male) decide; *you* (female) respond."[3]

Texts that affirm human dignity and "likeness to God" abound in scripture. My friend Teresa reminds us that many hymns and songs of faith also declare that we all *deserve* to be treated with respect, e.g., "Love Divine," "O Christ, the Healer," and "Spirit of Gentleness." Such affirmations pour out of the literature of faith. They are magnificent reminders to anyone on the journey toward restored dignity that no amount of body or mind battering can break the spirit. Scripturally, "mending" *is* the last word.

I found me

Wanda, on the other hand, did not find the healing path within church circles. Quite to the contrary, after being awakened to the abusive nature of her marriage, and despite knowing that some women she knew were greatly helped in faith-centred groups and in worship, she found the church milieu stifling. In the particular congregation to which she belonged, male exclusive language was always used in Sunday services. The two male ministry staff oriented all their preaching around traditional "service in the world" and "Jesus as achiever" themes. She did not hear a word to Wanda — a woman needing to hear about the mending message of the gospel.

Even though she loved her church dearly, she nonetheless began to feel that she was being *further damaged* within the church environment. She made an appointment to speak with one of the ministers, who told her that it wasn't unusual for women her age (seventy-one) to feel lost in today's world. Her husband Tony was a well-meaning, if crabby, sort and, if she just hung in there, she'd pull out of her slump.

That was the last straw. She met with me because she had heard me say in a local radio interview that the restoration of dignity following wife abuse might happen within church or non-church circles. With genuine curiosity she asked, why did a minister feel that, for some people, "finding herself" might happen in the secular world? My response was to suggest reading *Women Who Run with the Wolves* in which the recovery of self-esteem is set out in terms of mythical and psycho-therapeutic images, not in the language of the Bible. In our most recent conversation, Wanda described it as the single most important book she had ever read.

Women Who Run with the Wolves by Clarissa Pinkola Estes, is about rediscovering one's "wild nature." As Estes uses the term, wild does not mean untamed or unruly, but "wild" as in natural or uncaptured. Estes is a Jungian psychoanalyst and storyteller, who identifies in the myths of many cultures the great themes of loss and rediscovery of self. In Estes' terms, a girl's "wild" is overtaken and subjugated in very early childhood by countless cultural and familial demands. A girl loses her autonomous self by handing it over. As a little girl one learns what poses to strike in which social settings. Following the approved script continues into adolescence and into marriage: this is what a bride looks like; this is how a wife behaves; this is how you mother children; this is how you satisfy your husband.

Estes maintains that such relinquishing of one's wild nature is universal. The question for every woman is, "When will I begin the arduous task of being who I want to be?" This is the task of recovering the "wild woman"; the task of releasing her, freeing her from cultural or religious taboos telling her who she should be and what she should do.

> When women reassert their relationship with the wildish nature, they are gifted with a permanent and internal watcher, a knower, a visionary, an oracle, an inspiratrice, an intuitive, a maker, a creator, an inventor, and a listener who guide, suggest, and urge vibrant life in the inner and outer worlds. So, the word wild here is not used in its modern pejorative sense, meaning out of control, but in its original sense, which means to live a natural life, one in which the *criatura*, creature, has innate integrity and healthy boundaries."[4]

If a sense of dignity and self-respect has been damaged by extended hurt from one's intimate partner, these gifts of the inner life seem remote indeed. Life feels far from vibrant. Natural creative/knowing/visionary traits have been squeezed out, deflated. With therapeutic support and guidance, and a little help from one's friends, one can redefine one's self-concept: "I am as I should be; I am responsible for my own sense of dignity, my zest for life, my integrity; no one shall ever again take them away."

> Having a lover/friend who regards you as a living growing *criatura*, ...one that is human but made of very fine and moist and magical things as well ... these are the people you are looking for. They will be the friends of your soul for life. Mindful choosing of friends and lovers, not to mention teachers, is critical to your remaining conscious, remaining intuitive, remaining in charge of the fiery light that sees and knows.[5]

Wanda found *Women Who Run with the Wolves* a powerful stimulus to recovering her self-esteem in the face of long-standing "passive abuse." Her husband, Tony, had long since quit caring about her. He was silent for days, and often emerged only to express a complaint or criticism. Not long into their marriage (forty-eight years ago) she began to sense that nothing that she did mattered at all to him. If she expressed an opinion, he said, "Oh, well that's your view." There was no dialogue, only dismissive apathy. When she was ill, or when she was perplexed by what decision to make in the face of a life issues, he only looked at her with vacant eyes. Some of his looks even communicated loathing for her, and if she expressed her hurt he only said, "Dummy up, lady!" It was his stock retort to any attempt at serious sharing of her feelings.

Wanda and Tony have two children, now in their thirties. They are fully aware of the parents' cold and empty relationship, but when Wanda sought comfort from them, they both replied with a brusque, "Mom, you're as bad as him, you know; and anyway, it's just the way he is."

Wanda had left Tony four times in the eight years before we met, but returned home each time on the advice of close friends and the insistence of her children: "Dad needs somebody to look after him, and you *did* promise on your wedding day." After all, he was not being "abusive," so why not just put up with him; she wasn't the first person to have a sullen spouse.

Women Who Run with the Wolves has made Wanda giddy with optimism. She knows that her happiness does not depend on Tony's moods. She knows she cannot change him. He does not interfere with her social life, mainly bridge club every Friday afternoon. Her steadily deepening conviction is that she can listen to her heart, and that "advice" from friends or family is not necessary.

"They don't have to throw rescue ropes to me anymore," Wanda said to me recently. "I even think I'll be a better friend and mother. As for Tony, well I wish I could help him with whatever has been chewing at him all these years. For now I'll keep letting my *wild* become free."

"Wanda," I said, "it sounds like you're saying that you'll be living *around* Tony, not *with* him."

"Yes," she said, "I guess that's the way it has to be. I don't want to leave him. There's no other man in my life. And I can't wait to see what's around the next corner of life."

Seventy-one, going on twenty-one. Wanda is mending and anticipating, not blaming.

Another way of "finding yourself" is through writing. Keeping a journal or writing poetry can help anyone deal with their most disturbing experiences and get in touch with their deepest feelings. In this way, writing things down enables you to "close a chapter" in your life and move on to the next part of the story. Writing is a form of private therapy that doesn't require any bravery or psychotherapy or even writing skills. It just requires a problem to be worked out. When the problem is down on paper you can examine it, learn from it, distance yourself from it, do something about it, change the ending, and so on.

The following poem has been hoarded away as a treasure of mine. It has been read over and over again and is coffee-stained from overuse. I don't know who wrote it, but it is an excellent example of a writer dealing with the disappointments and pain in her life. Writing it down means working it out.

Comes the Dawn

After a while you learn the subtle difference
Between holding a hand and chaining a soul,
And you learn that love doesn't mean leaning
And company doesn't mean security,
And you begin to learn that kisses aren't contracts
And presents aren't promises,
And you begin to accept your defeats
With your head up and your eyes open,
With the grace of a woman, not the grief of a child,

And learn to build all your roads
On today because tomorrow's ground
Is too uncertain for plans, and futures have
A way of falling down in mid-flight.
After a while you learn that even sunshine
Burns if you get too much.
So you plant your own garden and decorate
Your own soul, instead of waiting
For someone to bring you flowers.
And you learn that you really can endure...
That you really are strong
And you really do have worth.
And you learn and learn...
With every good-bye you learn.

The problem wasn't me after all!

Of course professional therapy has many benefits too. Talking it out with a trained listener is another good way of working through problems. Helen saw a therapist weekly for about two years after she decided not to tolerate any longer a marriage consumed by her husband's obsessive sexual demands. They had been married about twelve years, and had three children. Her husband Roy had inherited from his own father an "I'm in charge" mentality, which expressed itself in an insatiable sexual appetite. "When I want it, how I want it" was his slogan, and his idea of sexual intimacy was to gratify himself — quickly. He never asked Helen what might give her sexual pleasure. As she put it later, "I am ashamed to put it this way, but my body was little more than a masturbating device. During my period he hardly talked to me."

Roy refused marital counselling, saying that the problem was her lack of sexual adventure. "Maybe if we tried two-couple sex. I'm kind of curious. What about it?"

This was the last straw. She knew that her sense of self was going down the tubes. It wasn't that Roy's sexual thoughtlessness in itself was destroying her. Rather her image of herself as little more than a faceless device was pushing her to the brink of despair.

Helen entered into private therapy before deciding to separate. After only a few sessions she knew that the recovery of her sense of worth as a woman could not take place in partnership with Roy.

Her friends and her children could not fathom why she should want to leave the marriage. (How could they? They knew nothing of what went on behind the bedroom door). The therapeutic journey was arduous at first, but after one particularly intense session she knew she had made the turn.

She was more self-assured than she'd been in years, more confident that decisions she made were right. Her daughter and two sons were the first to notice. It wasn't that she felt wonderful every day, but after only a few months of rigorous psychotherapy she was on a healing path. After two years she and her therapist agreed that the sessions could end, with the possibility of return at any time.

"Spirit, Spirit of Gentleness"

I met Shirley many years ago in northern Ontario; her church became her safe place. This song became her mantra:

> Spirit, Spirit of gentleness,
> blow thro' the wilderness calling and free,
> Spirit, Spirit of restlessness,
> stir me from placidness,
> Wind, Wind on the sea.[6]

Shirley had virtually memorized this still popular 70's song by James K. Manley, which became a kind of theme song for the women's support group in her congregation. They had not deliberately done so; it was just that someone always asked that they begin their meeting by singing it. The group conducted the worship service one Sunday, and after speaking about recovery after abuse, they closed with "Spirit, Spirit of Gentleness." That service was one of the most moving that I and many others in the congregation had ever experienced. To this day whenever I sing that song an image of that tiny group of women bravely leading that service leaps to my mind. And I weep softly, as they and many others did that Sunday.

For Shirley, the women's support group was the warm setting in which her self-respect was nourished. Most people had no idea what had squeezed the sense of worth out of her soul, but it was evident that the dynamic of the group was helping her form new visions of who Shirley was and could be. In many ways she exemplified the spirit of gentleness of which they sang.

Congregations can become sanctuaries where women who have been hurt at home can find a listening ear and support for the healing journey. One of the major reasons why a congregation provides a unique kind of mending support is its prayer and biblical base. This can make a tremendous difference to many hurt people. Self-help support groups need not have such a base; the support comes from the participants. Psychotherapeutic counsel need not, and typically does not, have such an explicitly spiritual base; many people find professional therapy essential to overcoming their problems.

Despite my great regard for the healing potential in such approaches as Estes', my own conviction is that a spiritual dimension to healing provides mending for the soul, as well as the mind. The damaging of dignity that results from home-based assault can be so total, so spirit-destructive that, in my view, nothing short of the awesome re-creative power of God can reach the deepest places in the heart that cry out for mending. Many women have told me that the spiritual base of a congregational group or of personal meditation was crucial to their return to wholeness.

Those in church leadership roles become quite accustomed to contacting an outside agency or "specialist" resource in the community — such as a shelter — for advice or referral. If a congregation and its ministry staff have made an attempt to join in the community-wide response to wife abuse, the networking goes both ways. I have received referral calls from community agencies on behalf of women who want to discuss issues of faith specifically. Such discussions usually revolve around guilt, forgiveness, or divorce. In our pastoral counselling sessions, such questions as these usually arise:

- Does God care?
- Does God hear my cry?
- Should I forgive the one who hurt me?
- Is divorce a sin?
- Why do I feel that when things go wrong, it's my fault?

In essence, what these women want to know is, "Can I be the woman who touches Jesus' garments?" A congregation that cheers on and intentionally ministers with women who are renewing their lives can play a key role in helping them reach for those spiritual answers.

Chapter 10

Real Male Strength and the Dignity of Tenderness

> What then are we to say? Should we continue in sin in order that grace may abound? By no means! How can we who died to sin go on living in it? Do you not know that all of us who have been baptized into Christ Jesus were baptized into his death? Therefore we have been buried with him by baptism into death, so that, just as Christ was raised from the dead by the glory of the Father, so we too might walk in newness of life.
>
> — Romans 6:1-4

And men, what of you and me? What are our healing paths? If you have seen any part of yourself mirrored in this book, what then? In our own ways we too cry, we hope someone will respond, and we pray for mending which will draw fragments of the soul together.

Don't ask me now what I think of you

Not long ago a man telephoned me and said: "Hi, I'm Steve. You don't know me. My minister, Grace, suggested I call you... I need help. Last week I hit my wife for the first time ever.... Please, could we talk?"

I went to Steve's home, and met an agitated six-foot-two executive in his fifties. "Agnes, my wife, knew you were coming over; she's gone shopping to let us talk alone. My God, in twenty-seven years of marriage I've never..."

He broke down in tears. Five minutes later he was able to continue. He spoke of the shock on Agnes' face when he slammed his fist against her shoulder. It had taken her a few moments for it to register that he had struck her, then she ran from the room sobbing. Steve had sat down and stared at the TV for an hour, not really believing that he'd hit the woman he said he loved. The shoulder was bruised black. They had long since been empty-nesters, since their only daughter was married with a family, and living in another part of town. For two days they didn't speak to one another. He broke the ice on the third day, when he said to Agnes, "Do you think Grace could help me? She's talked about family violence in a couple of sermons. What would she think of me? Agnes, what do *you* think of me?"

Silence. Then, "Don't ask me right now. I'm seeing a women's support group leader tonight. I'm doing what *I* have to do. You do what you have to do. But this is the wrong time to ask me what I think of you."

I asked him to tell me what had been happening in his life. He told me that for some time he had been on Agnes' case for any little thing she did that was not to his liking. He expected dinner on the table at six, fresh shirts ironed and pants pressed for his work day, and "peace and quiet" in the evening so he could cool out after the day's business stress. For at least five years he had insisted that none of Agnes' friends visit in the evening. Phone calls were okay, if they were short, but he admitted that he always sat close by so he'd know who she was talking to and on what subjects. He'd told Agnes frequently that her friends were losers. As for parties — they had not been to a social evening with other couples for ages.

I asked Steve how he would "name" the behaviours he had just described to me. He didn't understand. I did not try to categorize the dismissive ways in which he had been treating Agnes for a long time, but after a bit more probing, he did. He admitted, with genuine shock and shame, that he'd been abusing Agnes for years. He had never thought that manipulation of his wife's life in all the ways he could now identify were serious emotional torture. Furthermore, I ventured, it is quite possible that Agnes will lay an assault charge against you. "But why?" he asked with alarm. "This was the first time I hit her!" "Steve," I said, "what you did is a criminal act. You have *named* your deed and what led up to it as the abuse that it was; now realize that it is against the law to hit someone — anyone."

After my seeing Steve twice, he called a local counselling agency and signed up for a men's group for further, long-term help. That one particular church-attending male was prepared to look hard at the way he was damaging his wife — and had been for years. I hope he is moving toward a rebirth day, as a changed man.

A word of caution here: Steve's *intention* was to change, and he was regarding a men's group process as the vehicle for that change. But men's groups in which abusive males take part do *not* have a good reputation. There have been so many examples of men who diligently attend such groups becoming *more* abusive afterwards that women in the shelter movement are generally skeptical about their value. In fact, some shelter people reject outright the notion of groups for abusive men.

What, then, is their answer? Jail. After the first time. *That* is a consequence a man can understand. I do not share this skepticism, and later in the chapter will say something about the kinds of safeguards that can be built into group work with men.

By this point men may feel quite exhausted by the succession of "cry" stories, and "response" strategies. The common thread throughout has been the ways in which men have hurt their wives with a greater or lesser degree of intent, severity, and consequence. We must now ask the question, "What am I as a man prepared to do to stop the abuse?" Let's be "man" enough not to hide behind relative responses such as "I'm not as bad as my neighbour," or "Compared to the stories in this book, our home is a paradise; we have *none* of the scenes in 'Cry'."

Fair enough. It is always possible to compare one's own attitudes or actions to those of others, and come out *relatively* blameless in one's own eyes. But the purpose of the book has not been to point out the mind-sets and behaviour of *some* men, and be satisfied with moral judgment. My view is that *all* males share a number of such potential abusive characteristics. Only you will know which ones they are. Only you will know what parts of you have to "die to sin" so as to be lifted to "newness of life" (Romans 6:2-4).

Before there can be any movement toward zero tolerance of violence against women, including one's wife, men must take stock of their own view of women and *put to death* the mind-sets we described in Chapter 1. Not soften them. Not eliminate some and tolerate others. Get rid of *all* those attitudes which pave the way for the mental torture, physical abuse, and sexual domination of women.

Before offering practical suggestions on how that might be done, I want once again to present a faith-setting. The "death" we are talking about here only makes sense as part of our whole-life understanding of discipleship. These facets of faith apply particularly to men.

A theology of self-emptying

The technical term for such a theology is kenosis, which means "emptying." Kenotic theology is a particular view of Jesus in relation to God, namely that he emptied himself of power in order that he might express in vulnerability the deep serving love of God.[1] It is an incarnation theology in which a statement about Jesus is understood to be a reflection of the nature of God.

Paul sets forth such a "Christology" (theory of Christ's nature) in Philippians 2:5-11. It is generally seen as a hymn of the early church, in which the belief that Jesus emptied himself of power to enter fully into vulnerability was elevated to some kind of liturgical (even hymn-like) status:

> Let the same mind be in you that was in Christ Jesus,
> who, though he was in the form of God,
> did not regard equality with God
> as something to be exploited
> but emptied himself, [*heauton ekenosen*]
> taking the form of a slave,
> being born in human likeness.

And being found in human form,
he humbled himself
and became obedient to the point of death
even death on a cross.

Therefore God also highly exalted him
and gave him the name
that is above every name,
so that at the name of Jesus
every knee should bend,
in heaven and on earth and under the earth,
and every tongue should confess
that Jesus Christ is Lord,
to the glory of God the father.

The challenge to men is this: In faithful reflection on your being a friend of Jesus, who emptied himself of power, are you prepared to empty yourself of those power mind-sets and actions by which you have hurt women?

So simple. So complex.

Woman abuse is basically about the abuse of power. Men do not hurt women because they have "lost control" of themselves, but because they are attempting to assert control. An abusive husband preemptively assumes for himself patriarchal rights out of which flow the tactics of manipulation, coercion, and even assault.

Patriarchy is bred into the mind-set of every male in much the same way that the "wild woman" is bred out of every female. The ability to break free from these cultural patterns is essential to both men and women. A denial of patriarchy will enable men to become more fully themselves and will enable them to establish real and lasting partnerships with women. Changes in mind-set and behaviour signal a death of the old self and rebirth as a new man who is radically renewed in his understanding of who he is as a husband, and who his wife is as a woman.

The death of the old self is redemptive only for the man himself. It will not "save" his wife — it may not even save his marriage — but it will be critical for a man's own mending, just as forgiveness is integral to healing.

Such a challenge invites a husband who has to any degree whatever exercised authority over his wife — and seen her as responsible to him — to step aside. Her healing will be without his direct input. He is called to take responsibility for his own healing. He is called to a total self-emptying of all such oversight and supervisory prerogatives, and to a totally fresh recognition of his vulnerabilities.

He is called to be there *with* her and *for* her, but not *over* her. In Jesus' words of radical kenosis, "I am among you as one who serves" (Luke 22:27).

Men who have striven to be masters in their own homes would do well to consider the alternate model of maleness as expressed in Jesus' life of servanthood. True male strength lies not in muscles or in fists but in empathy and gentleness. In the words of one contemporary songwriter, "What does it take to be a man? What does it take to see it's a heart and soul, a gentle hand...."[2]

In the fifties and sixties, when I was being trained and was serving my first pastoral charges, "servanthood" was a very popular way of describing the essence of Christian discipleship for both women and men. In the seventies female theologians and church leaders began to identify the cruel irony of inviting women — who were already seen in the church in essentially servant roles — to servanthood. The proper identification of servant theology as a *captivating*, and not a *freeing* goal of Christian discipleship for women was among the early trademarks of feminist theology.

There is strength in servanthood, however, for both sexes. Mother Theresa is a prime example of a strong and powerful woman who sees herself as a servant of God and of humankind. If servanthood is chosen freely, it is not a signal of weakness, but a sign of strength. Unfortunately women have been thrust into serving roles — serving husband, children, and church — without being served in return. It is time for men to shift their own behaviour from that of master to that of servant.

Personal inventory: a lesson from AA

The programme of Alcoholics Anonymous also sets out a whole-life process of personal change and re-evaluation of attitudes that is instructive in our attempt to find the mending required for abusive men. The twelve steps of AA have become a blueprint for self-help groups everywhere. Note particularly the fourth and tenth steps: to make — and continue to make — a searching and fearless moral inventory of oneself.

THE TWELVE STEPS OF AA

1. We admitted we were powerless over alcohol — that our lives had become unmanageable.
2. Came to believe that a Power greater than ourselves could restore us to sanity.
3. Made a decision to turn our will and our lives over to the care of God as we understood [God].
4. Made a searching and fearless moral inventory of ourselves.
5. Admitted to God, to ourselves, and to another human being the exact nature of our wrongs.
6. Were entirely ready to have God remove all these defects of character.
7. Humbly asked [God] to remove our shortcomings.
8. Made a list of all the persons we had harmed, and became willing to make amends to them all.
9. Made direct amends to such people wherever possible, except when to do so would injure them or others.
10. Continued to take personal inventory and when we were wrong promptly admitted it.
11. Sought through prayer and meditation to improve our conscious contact with God as we understood [God], praying only for knowledge of [God's] will for us and the power to carry that out.
12. Having had a spiritual awakening as the result of these steps, we tried to carry this message to alcoholics and to practice these principles in all our affairs.[3]

Stopping drinking is a whole-life process in the AA programme. Many alcoholic men and women have tried to quit "cold turkey" on their own. For some, it works, for others, it is to no avail. Without the back-up resources of a whole-life programme and a weekly fellowship base many have discovered that they just can't "go it alone." Furthermore, it is not realistic to expect that deeply ingrained patterns of abusive drinking — and usually abusive behaviour along with it — will end by a simple "desire" to quit.

A recognition of that fact drove Bill W. and Dr. Bob to found Alcoholics Anonymous in 1935.[4] They recognized that it is the destructive life patterns and attitudes out of which abusive drinking arises that need attention, and any member of the programme will tell you that working on those patterns and attitudes is a life-long commitment. They will also tell you that if one gets stuck at the "I've quit drinking — hooray" stage and refuses to examine the underlying pattern and attitude dynamics of their addiction, they are not "working the programme." The result is usually a continuation of the abusive behaviour, even though the drinking has stopped. Such a person is a "dry drunk," sober, but still acting out "as if" drunk. Still hurting those around him or her.

If a man recognizes himself in *any* of the stories or abusive mind-set attitudes that have been set out in this book, then he is a prime candidate for a "searching and fearless moral inventory." Even if one has already stopped recognizable abusive behaviour, but still privately harbours old attitudes about male headship, an inventory is a must. But, as with ending alcoholism, a man must first develop the will to change.

No more back-handers!

Phil ended his physical abuse of Angie — "a back-hander now and again," as he put it — five years ago after Angie told a teacher, then, a few days later, myself, about what was going on. After being informed that she had blown the whistle on his violence, Phil agreed to meet with me within days.[5]

In our first meeting Phil expressed genuine shame at the abusive routines he had fallen into, and vowed that he would never hit his wife again. But he also recognized in that first conversation together that what now needed urgent attention was his incredibly deep-seated "I'm-the-boss" attitude. Within a month, he and two other men in the congregation I was then serving were meeting on a weekly basis in my home. Three other men later joined us, and for three years we continued to meet regularly. The seven of us helped one another to peal off protective skins of denial and naïveté. Over time we all discovered that, to some degree, we all shared assumptions of male superiority and that we had said and done things to our wives which were unquestionably abusive.

As the level of trust deepened, we were able to identify some specifics and, inevitably, the discussion turned to the underlying "male headship" mind-set which we had all brought into our marriages. A look at the Fifth Step of AA will clarify how a similar process may be identified in the deliberate change of abusive attitudes — of what must follow "personal inventory" for any man who wants to change. The Fifth Step requires that one "admit to God, to oneself, and to another human being the exact nature of our wrongs." This is a big step. Many members of AA have said that it is the most difficult for them; some never get beyond the Third. It is one thing to admit to yourself how your behaviour has hurt others, it is quite another to confess it to another person.

My own experience with men's groups has been quite positive and, with careful guidance, I think they can work. Men, as well as women, need to know that they are not alone; that others share their problems and their desire to find solutions. In small circles of six or seven, men can learn to trust and then to support one another in their quest to change the "male-headship" mind-set into a mutual partnership mind-set.

The danger in men's groups lies in the obvious pitfall that, instead of supporting change in each other, men will reinforce abusive behaviour. Group facilitators need to be carefully trained, wisely chosen, and able to spot and defuse any counter-productive tendencies. It is important to keep focused on the fact that a man cannot change for the sake of his wife, but must have the desire to change for himself — because it will make him a better person, not just a better husband.

Am I optimistic about male commitment to ending violence toward women? Yes and No. Yes, I do believe that there is a slow but discernible change in the willingness of many men to let their tender nature show. We live in a century in which maleness has typically been defined by military and athletic models. The point is to *win*, and it is the aggressive who win. The "win" model has its place, for an army or a ball team which was not aggressive, and did not care whether it won or lost, would be routed. But this model has no place behind the walls of home. I am convinced that more and more men believe that. The delicacy with which many young fathers play with and tend to their children is a consequence of the relatively recent sharing of parental opportunity and responsibility.

I predict that the "21st century man" will be even more in touch with his own tender heart, and therefore he'll be stronger.

But no, I am not optimistic about the near future. The majority of men cling to patriarchy, and have no desire to let go of the reins of control at home. "I decide" is still the male motto, but it conceals what some have called "the male wound" — a fundamental crack in the inner texture of boys and men. The notion of "original sin" is out of vogue in most theological circles, and only fundamentalist faith groups have stressed the necessity of being "born again" in recent decades. But the male tendency to control and hurt is so deep that only an image like rebirth is big enough to express the shape of a new maleness. Such rebirth is not only for individual males, but for church and community structures in which male prerogatives still prevail as well.

I began this book by asking men to wake up. I end by asking men to speak up, to announce publicly and in every way possible that the assault of women is criminal. Reject patriarchy and embrace partnership. Be "born again" to real strength, and to the dignity of tenderness.

However, individual action is not enough. The church too must wake up and speak up. The church too must reject patriarchy and embrace partnership. Jesus' message of active and gracious love must apply to male-female relationships as well as to our own relationships with Jesus and with God. Jesus' message "to love one another as I have loved you" (see John 13:34) does not include physical, emotional, or sexual abuse and the assertion that "love endures all things" does not mean that women should endure abuse. In essence, the church fails in its ministry when it fails to speak out on important social issues such as woman abuse and far too many women have already paid the price for that silence.

The phrase "domestic violence" — like "civil war" — is inherently contradictory. There is nothing "domestic" about violence nor "civil" about war but such phrases lull us into a false sense that such matters are "private" or "internal" and do not require our response. Both individuals and institutions must speak out and act to end such injustice. Women's rights, quite simply, are human rights and any attack against a woman is an attack against humanity. Women are not the perpetrators of woman abuse but, for the most part, they have been left to clean up the fall-out and deal with the problem. It is time for the rest of us to join them in ending the abuse and establishing new and joyful patterns of intimacy for the next millennia. When the words "domestic" and "violence" are no longer paired in our thinking, and women living with men are finally safe at home, then, at last, we can truly celebrate marriage as an expression of God's love at work on earth.

About the Author

Morton Paterson is a graduate of McMaster University (B.A. Hons.), the State University of Iowa (M.A.), and Emmanuel College (B.D.). He was ordained a minister of The United Church of Canada in 1963 and served the Mindemoya Pastoral Charge on Manitoulin Island for three years. He then returned to university to complete Ph.D. studies in philosophy at the University of Toronto. He taught philosophy at Laurentian University for twelve years, wrote for church publications, and did research in the history of philosophy in Canada.

In 1984 Morton became the first recipient of the McGeachy Memorial Senior Scholarship, and for two years he had an opportunity to study the church's ministry with victims and offenders both in Canada and abroad. His research resulted in the publication of *Toward a Justice That Heals* (Toronto: The United Church Publishing House, 1988).

In 1987 he began a four-year ministry at East Plains United Church, Burlington, where he helped to form a "Family Justice Committee." In 1991 he took a half-time position at Melrose United Church in Hamilton in order to have time for research and writing, and in January 1993 he retired early in order to devote full time to family violence ministry.

Morton Paterson was born in Unity, Saskatchewan, and raised in Sudbury, Ontario. He has been married twice, is a father and grandfather, and lives on a farm near Uxbridge, Ontario. He also enjoys being an amateur radio operator and a classical guitarist.

Notes

Foreword by Don Gillies

1 Quoted in Peter Rutter, *Sex in the Forbidden Zone* (New York: Ballantine Books, 1989): frontispiece.

2 Marie M. Fortune, "The Nature of Abuse," in *Pastoral Psychology*, Vol. 41, No. 5 (May 1993): 279.

3 Elly Danica, *Don't: A Woman's Word* (Charlottetown: gynergy books, 1988).

4 Sam Keen, *Fire in the Belly* (New York: Bantam Books, 1991): 42-43.

5 Guy Corneau, *Absent Fathers, Lost Sons* (Boston: Shambhala Publications, 1991): 120.

6 Fortune, p. 275.

Preface

1 Marshall and Vaillancourt, *Changing the Landscape*, p. 10.

2 All but the last of these statistics are highlights of the Women's Safety Project, a community-based study in Toronto that was already in progress when the Panel on Violence Against Women was appointed. The statistics are quoted in *Changing the Landscape* Executive Summary, p. 11. For more information, see Randall and Haskell under "Journals" in Appendix II. For more information on murder statistics see Chapter 6, footnote 1.

3 Literally, I Corinthians 11:24 does not contain the word "broken." The New Revised Standard Version, for example, reads, "This is my body, that is for you." Nor do any of the synoptic gospel accounts (Matthew 26:26, Mark 14:22, Luke 22:19) refer to "my body broken." The Gospel of John does not speak of the bread and wine at all; rather Jesus is described as washing the feet of the disciples (13:1-11). Why, then, does the liturgical tradition have Jesus saying "Take, eat, this is my body, which is *broken* for you; this do in remembrance of me?" Some early Greek manuscripts contained the word *klomenon*, derived from *klao*, which means to break into pieces; early descriptions of home communion preferred this version (Acts 2:46, 20:7, 27:35). The pilgrims on the road to Emmaus recognized the risen Jesus in the breaking of bread (Luke 24:30), and in his caution against celebrating the last supper in a compromising party atmosphere, Paul says, "The bread that we break, is it not a sharing in the body of Christ?" (I Corinthians 10:16b). The book title, therefore, evokes early church liturgy rather than the "last words" as recorded in the gospels.

4 *Dr. Jesus,* based on the wholeness ministry of Jesus, was published privately by the author in 1993.

5 For a fascinating account of the non-coercive ways in which Jesus used power read the sociological study by Jay Haley, *The Power Tactics of Jesus Christ, and Other Essays,* (New York: Grossman Publishers, 1969).

6 Dyke, *Crucified Woman,* pp. 63-64.

7 For a good discussion of the impact of childhood trauma in the home, read Jehu and Gazan, "Psycho-social Adjustment of Women who were Sexually Victimized in Childhood or Adolescence," available from Health Canada (see "Sources" in Appendix II). Here is an example of one finding:

> Oppressed and demoralized wives who are victims themselves are in a poor position to instruct and equip their daughters to avoid these hazards. Thus the daughters of incapacitated mothers may well grow up to be incapacitated mothers themselves, daughters will in turn be vulnerable to sexual victimization ... [I]t follows that every effort is required to break this cycle of victimization by helping women victims to function more adequately as mothers, as well as modifying the supremacy of males in our society that may be facilitating the excessively dominant role adopted by many of the fathers concerned. (pp. 6-7)

Chapter 1

1 "The Violence Against Women Survey," Statistics Canada, p. 1 (See Appendix III)

2 For further information see "White Ribbon Campaign" and "Men Walking Against Male Violence" under "Sources" in Appendix II.

3 Most marriage services still contain a variation of the rubric:

> The minister shall say, "Who gives this woman to be married to this man?"
>
> The father, or whoever in his place, shall answer, "I do."

Many ministers recommend to marriage couples that they replace this "property transaction" anachronism with something like:

> The minister shall say in turn to the parent(s) of both bride and groom, "Do you give your blessing to the marriage of your daughter (son) to this man (woman), and do you welcome him (her) into your family?"
>
> The parent(s) shall say in turn, "We do."

4 The work of Eva Lundgren is referred to at some length in Chapter 8, but here I would like to quote one section of her unpublished paper, "I Am Endowed with All the Power in Heaven and on Earth":

> A theology which requires mankind to be small for God to be large needs, even requires, that "God" be male. Why? Because the hierarchical structure, with a large distance between "God" and mankind could not be maintained with a female image of "God." Our culture has no concepts, metaphors or reality for a "dominion of woman" — "Lord," in religious terms, has no female counterpart. (p. 8)

5 McDill and McDill, *Shattered and Broken*, p. 98.

6 Lois Wilson, a former Moderator of The United Church of Canada, in *Telling Her Story* (Toronto: The United Church Publishing House, 1992) invites readers of the Bible to

> [u]ncover and expose the role of women in biblical texts as enablers and supporters of a patriarchal society.... The all-giving mother, the public-pleasing woman have also been approvingly presented in ways that support patriarchy. Independent women like Abigail, David's wife, are written out of the narrative. (pp. 45-46)

7 See Letha Scanzoni and Bette Evans Wells, "Make Sure Your Counsellor is a Feminist," *Daughters of Sarah*, May/June 1980 (Chicago, Daughters of Sarah). This anecdote from the article illustrates the need for caution in the selection of a clergy counsellor:

> Laura... had begun to observe and question inequities in how women are treated in evangelical circles.... Feeling a need to discuss her thoughts with someone, she went to her pastor. "The problem," he said, "is that you don't have a man to guide you. That's why you are moving off base. These teachings on women's place are revealed in the Word and are *settled*." (p. 8)

8 In *The Stone Angel* (Toronto: Bantam, 1964), Margaret Laurence describes Bram's pitiful decline, part of which involved the following scenario:

> Bram referred to me as "that woman," like hired help, when he spoke of me to John. In the night, once only, I heard him call — "*Hagar!*" I went to his room, but he was only talking in his sleep. (p. 162)

9 The Church Council on Justice and Corrections (CCJC) has produced a fine resource on the corrosive impact of patriarchy, entitled *Family Violence in a Patriarchal Culture*. One section of the analysis is called "Naming the Culprit." See "Sources" in Appendix II for more information.

Chapter 2

1 In *Without Wings* (Charlottetown: gynergy books, 1993), a book about lesbian intimacy by Jackie Manthorne, Kate has the following thoughts after having been physically and sexually assaulted by her intimate friend, Maxine:

> She felt so ashamed. How had her relationship with Maxine come to blows? What had she done wrong? ... Deep down, she knew that it hadn't been her fault. She hadn't asked to be punched, and she hadn't asked to be raped.... What Maxine had done was unfathomable, reprehensible, and entirely her own responsibility. Still, it was hard not to second-guess, and she couldn't help but wonder if she had somehow provoked Maxine. Perhaps she did share part of the blame. Perhaps if she had done things differently, it wouldn't have happened. (p. 72)

2 This brief note appeared in *The Globe & Mail*, December 14, 1993, picked up from a Reuters news release from London, England:

> Most British women drivers believe they are as good behind the wheel as men, but nearly half suffer constant criticism from their male partners, a survey says. A survey of *She* magazine readers found almost ninety percent of women drivers say they are as competent at driving as men, but nearly two-thirds say their partner thinks he is the better driver. Nearly fifty percent say their men constantly criticize their performance.

3 In *Untying the Knot*, Roderick Phillips notes that some of the obstetrical literature in Ireland early in the twentieth century "often mentioned in passing that women miscarried after being beaten: 'The doctors were not particularly distressed by wife-beating, but mentioned it casually along with other medical details.'" (See Appendix IV).

4 Bohn, "Domestic Violence and Pregnancy." Bohn identifies studies from which she gleans these statistics, and notes others which indicate that

- one-third of a particular subject group reported abuse during all three trimesters of pregnancy
- subjects reported an average of 4.5 beatings during each pregnancy (p. 98)

5 Quoted with permission.

6 Abused Aboriginal women have had an opportunity to tell their stories in *Voices of Aboriginal Women*, produced by the Canadian Council on Social Development and the Native Women's Association of Canada. The quote is from page 6 of that volume. See "Sources" in Appendix II for more information.

In pre-marriage counselling in which one or both of the individuals is marrying for a second time, I ask, "Only if you are willing to answer the question, was there abuse in your first marriage?" If the answer is "No," then we leave the subject. About one-third of the women say, "Yes, and it's okay to talk about it; we already have." (No man has yet answered the question.) I then invite further discussion to the extent that the couple wishes to do so. If the abuse began before the wedding I ask, "Did you witness abuse in your home as you were growing up?" The answer to this question has always been "Yes." Normally I meet a couple four times before a wedding ceremony, but when abuse issues are raised we have additional meetings. On occasion I have recommended that one or both individuals seek further professional counselling.

7 I am grateful to Denis L. Parent, a student-at-law with the firm of Monteith, Baker, and Howe in Newmarket, Ontario for his assistance in locating the three sections of the Criminal Code of Canada that have direct bearing on stalking.

8 See "Mothers on Trial" under "Sources" in Appendix II.

Chapter 3

1 In Margaret Laurence's *The Stone Angel*, Bram Shipley facetiously offers his new bride, Hagar, the choice of "where" but not "whether":

> "Let's see what you look like under all that rig-out, Hagar."
> I look at him not so much in fear as in an iron incomprehension.
>
> "Downstairs" — he said. "Is that what bothers you? Or daylight? Don't fret — there's no one around for five miles."
> ... "I don't give a good goddamn. Hagar — you're my wife."
>
> It hurt and hurt, and afterward he stroked my forehead with his hand.
>
> "Didn't you know that's what's done?" (p. 44)

2 "The Violence Against Women Survey," Statistics Canada. See Appendix III.

3 Women's Safety Project, as quoted in *Changing the Landscape* Executive Summary, p. 11. For more information, see Randall and Haskell under "Journals" in Appendix II.

Chapter 4

1 Morgenson, Donald F., "Steel Dolls: Resilient Children in Tough Circumstances," *Growth Spurts*, No. 44 (Spring 1994), pp. 15, 10. *Growth Spurts* magazine is available from Growth Spurts Publishing, P.O. Box 325, Stn. P, Toronto, Ontario, M5S 2S8, Canada.

2 The quotation is from the movie adaptation of *The Prince of Tides*, which was directed by Barbara Streisand. The novel, written by Pat Conroy, expresses it this way:

> I do not know, however, when my mother and my father began their long, dispiriting war against each other. Most of their skirmishes were like games of ringolevio, with the souls of their children serving as the ruined captured flags in their campaigns of attrition. Neither considered the potential damage when struggling over something as fragile and unformed as a child's life. (p. 5)

3 Bruce Taylor has told me that between the years of twelve and fifteen he was stable and did not offend — due to the fatherly influence of the coach of the Toronto (Don) Rowing Club, Mark Thompson. Bruce, twelve years old, and

two other boys had stolen money from the clubhouse locker room ($9). They were caught, and as a penalty Bruce was made to scrub floors at the club. Mark Thompson was a retired police officer, and took time to talk to him. After the scrubbing punishment ended he asked Bruce to be a coxswain for club races — a position that would require considerable travelling to races. For the first time ever Bruce was doing something that he felt good at, and to this day he credits that man as a key stabilizing influence. He has drawn on that self-esteem "well" many times since. Police officers, Guide and Scout Leaders, Elementary and High School (and Sunday School) teachers, and others who play such positive roles *in loco parentis* — especially if the atmosphere at home was toxic — seldom hear of the important influence they have on a child.

4 See Beaumont, "Promise Not to Tell," for an example which mirrors the triangulation which Janet experienced in her childhood:

> Maggie, 47, remembers her father complaining all her life, "Your mother doesn't love me. She wants to divorce me"; and her mother, in turn, reinforcing that notion by saying, "If I could get a decent job, I'd take control of my own life." Anticipating the divorce that never materialized (her parents recently celebrated their 50th wedding anniversary) "was like waiting for the other shoe to drop," says Maggie — and the specious confidences only served to undermine her sense of security and familial bonding. (p. 153)

Harriet Lerner also speaks of the long-lasting effects of a child being persuaded to keep secrets. In *The Dance of Deception.* "Linda," at the age of ten, inadvertently found out that she had an older brother who had died when he was a month old. Lerner says this of the secrecy scenario that developed when she later asked her mother about his death:

> ... Linda's mother asked her not to mention the subject to any other family members. There was no reason, she said, for Linda's younger sisters to know or for their father to be reminded of this loss because "your father can't handle difficult things." It was better, she explained, that he remain unaware that Linda even knew. (p. 141)

Chapter 5

1 The basic meaning of the Hebrew word *kabash* which is translated here as "ravished" is to subdue, bring into bondage, dominate, or force. It connotes extreme violence, certainly including being against the will of the victim.

2 I wince inside when the expression "love endures all things" from I Corinthians 13:7 is read, for on the surface it seems to be a licence for one partner to inflict anything which the other will endure. The verb in Greek is *hupomeno*, which means literally "to stay behind," suggesting the modern expression "to stick it out." In the context of persecution in which the early church found itself, such endurance was a willingness to suffer martyrdom:

> But recall those earlier days when, after you had been enlightened, you endured (*hupemeinate*) a hard struggle with sufferings, sometimes being publicly exposed to abuse and persecution... (Hebrews 10:32-33a)

It would be a gross misapplication of this text to suggest that this could include marital martyrdom, but combined with I Peter 3:1-2 (see page 77), the connection is not far-fetched.

3 Lerner, *The Dance of Anger*, pp. 2-3.

4 Amy Tan portrays such tragic desperation well in *The Joy Luck Club* (New York: Ivy Books, 1989):

> So I will tell Lena of my shame. That I was rich and pretty. I was too good for any one man. That I became abandoned goods. I will tell her that at eighteen the prettiness drained from my cheeks. That I thought of throwing myself in the lake like the other ladies of shame. And I will tell her of the baby I killed because I came to hate this man so much. (p. 281)

5 Lerner, *The Dance of Anger*, p. 26.

6 The concept of "I-statements" in dealing with one's own anger is covered in depth by Lerner in *The Dance of Anger* and was first introduced to me by Tammy McConnell. She and her husband, Andrew, had been introduced to the idea in a pre-marriage counselling course as an effective strategy for dealing creatively with anger. Tammy and I co-facilitated a workshop on anger at Trinity United Church, Beamsville in 1992. Even couples who had been married for many years agreed that this simple protocol could strengthen their marriages.

Chapter 6

1 The recent Statistics Canada report entitled "Spousal Homicide" notes:

- from 1974 through 1992, 1435 women and 451 men were slain by their spouses — an average of 17 victims per million couples per year.
- over the same period, a married woman was nine times as likely to be killed by her spouse as by a stranger.
- the rate of husbands killing wives is elevated in the aftermath of a separation.
- risk of spousal homicide is far greater in common-law marriages than in registered marriages, for both women and men.
- teenaged wives incur the greatest risk of being killed by their husbands.
- spousal homicide rates increase sharply as the age difference between wives and husbands increases.

The report concludes: "Killing of spouses constitutes a significant component of Canadian homicide: the 1886 women and men killed by spouses between 1974 and 1992 represent 15% of all Canadian homicide victims, 38% of adult female victims and 6% of adult male victims."

See Wilson and Daly, "Spousal Homicide," *Juristat.* Statistics quoted here are reproduced by authority of the Minister of Industry, 1994.

2 Most couples I marry still prefer the traditional vow:

> I, _____ take you, _____ to be my wife,
> to have and to hold from this day forward,
> for better, for worse;
> for richer, for poorer;
> in sickness and in health;
> in joy and in sorrow;
> to love and to cherish
> and to be faithful to you alone,
> as long as we both shall live.

Contrary to popular belief, the marriage ceremony has not for many years included "love, honour, and obey."

3 Quoted with permission.

4 Phillips, *Untying the Knot*, p. 102.

Chapter 7

1 Each of these episodes was rooted in a social attitude which we now recognize as cruel and unfair. It has been argued that the reason the children were being kept from Jesus was because they were orphans (hence not "fit" company), that any man so "caught" would be exonerated, and that the man's "dementia" was really epilepsy.

2 This section is a reprint (slightly revised) of "Where Truth Can be Told, Safely," which I wrote for *Vis-a-Vis.* I was gratified to receive requests for further information about "safe places" from a number of women's support agencies. See Appendix V for information on how to contact women's shelters.

3 The Church Council on Justice and Corrections (CCJC) has developed for congregational use a number of very practical resources both on how to educate on the issues and to inaugurate programmes for ministry with abused wives. See "Sources" in Appendix II for more information.

As an example of a special focus within an overall concern for ministry with victims of abuse in the family, the work of the Family Justice Committee of East Plains United Church, Burlington may be noted. While not losing a general support function, they now have a weekly meeting of Survivors of Incest Anonymous (SIA), with a loose affiliation with the national SIA network. For further information about two well established congregationally-based programmes, write to Family Justice Committee, East Plains United Church, 275 Plains Road

East, Burlington ON L7T 2C4 or Family Justice Committee, First United Church, 151 Lakeshore Road E., Mississauga ON L5H 1G3.

4 *Mandate*, Special Edition on the Ecumenical Decade of Churches in Solidarity with Women, The United Church of Canada, Vol. 22, No. 3, 1991, p. 31. This list was compiled by the Winnipeg Presbytery Task Group on Family Violence in their wife abuse protocol published in 1988. The Task Group went on to prepare a child abuse protocol, *Listen*, before disbanding in 1994.

5 White, "Wearing a Wife-Assault-Prevention Button," p. 1009.

6 Carrie Doehring is a minister of The Presbyterian Church in Canada now teaching Pastoral Care in the Divinity College of Boston University. Her Masters dissertation was called *The Dreams of Rape Victims*, and her doctoral dissertation was published by University Press of America under the title: *No Greater Desecration: Traumatization and Representations of God* (1993). She has given special attention to developing healing liturgies in the belief that worship has a unique power for those who have been victimized: the only reality great enough to answer the degradation of abuse is *divine*. Carrie has helped me to see that the spiritual community has a healing potential which is simply not available in secular approaches. One of the ways in which the church can partner with secular agencies is to add the dimension of prayer: "This kind can come out only through prayer." (Mark 9:29)

Chapter 8

1 From a transcript of a radio documentary first broadcast on June 19, 1985, on NKR Radio 2, and entitled "God is no tender man." The interview with Helene was produced by Lisa Strindberg and Kate Kartvelt, and translated into English by Eva Lundgren. Lundgren's book *I Herrens Vold* ("In the Grip of the Lord"), which includes an interview with Helene, was an elaboration of a research report she published in 1984 entitled (in English translation) "For the Lord Disciplines Her Whom He Loves."

2 In *The Dance of Deception*, Lerner says of the recent and healthier climate of truth-telling in the home:

> Family secrets appear to be private business, derived from the deepest interior of family life; but patriarchal injunctions promote silence and denial even about life-and-death matters, such as the horror and extent of male violence in women's lives. The cultural context determines not only which secrets can be told, but also which secrets can be remembered and which secrets can be heard ... However one understands it, something in the cultural emotional climate has shifted to allow for the honest memory and frank disclosure of even the most horrific of family secrets. (p. 154)

3 A 1990 publication of the prestigious Clarke Institute of Psychiatry in Toronto unfortunately maintains the silence. Its publication, *Marriage Counselling: An Information Guide* omits any direct reference to violence as a possible element

in family dysfunctionality. In 27 pages the closest it gets is an oblique reference in this Q/A couplet:

Q Is this just a phase we're going through or do we really need help?

A At one time or another all couples go through changes and stages and experience stress. How much stress each person can and is willing to tolerate at any particular time varies. If you feel your stress level is intolerable or that you have reached an impasse, you should seek help. (p. 9)

4 Another professional group that has broken the silence is The Women Teacher's Federation of Ontario. See Labatt under "Journals" in Appendix II for an excellent resource.

Chapter 9

1 If the abusing husband has been charged and dealt with in the courts then, to some extent, the burden has been shifted. In cases of woman assault or stalking I usually recommend that a charge be laid under the Criminal Code unless there are *serious* mitigating circumstances.

2 The phenomenon of the incestuous father becoming the ghostly "bed-mate" of his daughter years after the abuse has stopped is not unusual. It is now recognized as a major issue in counselling couples after a disclosure of incest has taken place.

3 Two other gospel stories are also rooted in unheard of female initiative and male response. In such accounts of Jesus' response to women the gospel writers show his disdain for the patriarchal code, by which males set the agendas for female behaviour.

In the first (Mark 7:24-30), Jesus was clearly nonplused when a Syrophoenician (foreign) woman asked him to help her epileptic daughter. His reply was, "Let the children [of Israel] be fed first, for it is not fair to take the children's food and throw it to the dogs." She persisted, "Sir, even the dogs under the table eat the children's crumbs." He relented, and cured the woman's daughter.

In the other (Luke 8:42b-48), a woman whose menstrual bleeding had not stopped in twelve years (menorrhagia) came to him in a crowd and touched his cloak, healing herself but rendering Jesus "unclean" by breaking an impurity code (Leviticus 15:19). Jesus said to her "Daughter, your faith has made you well; go in peace."

4 Estes, *Women Who Run with the Wolves*, p. 4.

5 *Ibid.*, p. 110.

6 James K. Manley, "Spirit, Spirit of Gentleness," *Songs for a Gospel People*, #108 (Winfield, B.C.: Wood Lake Books, 1971).

Chapter 10

1 My doctoral dissertation, *Radical Kenosis*, was a philosophical examination of one version of a so-called personalist view of God which maintains that God's nature, like ours, is subject to change over time. Some forms of Christian personalism make the further claim that changes in Jesus reflect changes in God. For example, Jesus' own willingness to relinquish or be emptied of (kenosis) power in favour of vulnerability somehow reflects a vulnerability in God.

2 Tom Scholz, "To Be a Man," on Boston, *Third Stage*, (Los Angeles: MCA Records, 1986).

3 Alcoholics Anonymous, *Twelve Steps and Twelve Traditions* (New York: Alcoholics Anonymous World Services Inc., 1952), p. 42. See also *Alcoholics Anonymous*, 3rd edition, (New York: Alcoholics Anonymous World Services Inc., 1976), which describes the origins and philosophy of AA and is referred to by members of the programme as "The Big Book." For specific information about AA contact a local chapter or the General Service Office of Alcoholics Anonymous, P.O. Box 459, Grand Central Station, New York, N.Y., 10163, U.S.A.

4 Driving down Main Street in downtown Hamilton one day I was trying to decipher the many stickers plastered across the trunk of the car in front of me. The first one my eye fastened on was "Honk if you Know Bill W." I didn't get it. Then I read two others, "Today is the First Day of the Rest of Your Life" and "Easy Does It," both popular AA slogans. As I passed the driver in the next lane I honked. He grinned at me and waved. Although I am not a member of the programme, Bruce Taylor has given me glimpses into the fellowship component in AA. Recently he gave me an "honorary medallion" representing twenty years of friendship.

5 I first met Helen and Phil through clergy networking. With Helen's permission, the teacher of whom I speak (call her Evelyn) asked her minister if she would meet with Helen, in order to work through her problems. Her minister demurred, but suggested my name. Helen agreed, I received the phone call, and within days Evelyn and Helen came to my office. Phil knew nothing of all this, and it turned out that his physical abuse was the tip of the iceberg. Within minutes in that first of many, many discussions Helen disclosed for the first time that she had been sexually assaulted by her father over a four-year period during her teen years. Phil knew nothing of this history either, and later became extremely angry that Helen had told Evelyn and myself before telling him. His anger at being "the last to know" prompted complex discussion at several meetings of the men's group of which we were both members. Evelyn, Helen, Phil and I have remained close friends. One offshoot of my many conversations with him has been a discovery that there is need for a focused men's group for the partners of incest survivors.

Appendix I
Suggestions for Study Groups

It used to be a relatively simple matter to distinguish between the "spiritual" and the "secular." In church settings like pulpit, Bible Study, youth or adult groups one discussed the spiritual. In a variety of community settings the themes were "secular."

How things have changed! We now recognize that the Bible is criss-crossed with passages that illuminate contemporary issues, particularly family issues. These study suggestions are intended to help church groups identify ways to end woman abuse and restore dignity to those who have been hurt. To be sure, the target audience for this book is you and me as individuals but, as so many self-help movements have shown, there is a special "extra" value in group struggle with hard issues. After all, abuse is not someone's personal problem; it indicates systemic social problems. The journey back to self-esteem requires both personal strengthening and a strengthening of interpersonal relationships for support and survival. What better way to explore the issues than in a setting where we can share insights based on our own experiences and help each other find ways to mend in community?

These suggestions for groups who use this book reflect many years of my own involvement with discussion groups. Hopefully they will stimulate ideas that will be useful to your particular group.

GENERAL SUGGESTIONS ABOUT A DISCUSSION GROUP

Size

A group from eight to ten is ideal — small enough to allow everyone a chance to speak, yet big enough to "permit" silence without awkwardness. This might be an established group within the church or one that is called together for special theme discussion. Members might choose to remain anonymous except to others in the group.

Gender mix

Mixed or one gender only? It really wouldn't matter. An all male or all female group could usefully discuss all of the themes addressed here. The ideal would be a mixed group, with some opportunity to divide into one gender sub-groups on occasion.

Facilitator

Male or female? Both or either. It would be a good idea to have two people responsible for planning the discussion series, with a division of responsibilities for each session. Having both a male and a female leader may be an especially useful tool for mixed groups, especially when one-gender sub-groups need leader input. The main role of the facilitator is to foster, not to control, the discussion. As long as the facilitator can plan the meetings, while allowing the group to explore in its own way, the question of gender should not be a problem. Remember, the group controls the agenda, not vice versa.

Goals

There may be some in the group whose wounds are still raw. It would be misleading (and potentially abusive) to assume that a discussion group could also be a therapy group. A self-help peer group can serve a healing function, and professionally guided group therapy is not always necessary or appropriate, but there is a fine line between them, which should not be crossed. There should be some attempt to articulate the goals of the group — both at the beginning and part-way through the series as a reality/comfort check.

Membership

Should the group consist only of people associated with the congregation? Normally an open group is best, and what better way to "do mission"? The community at large should know that your congregation is trying to deal with woman abuse directly. This would identify your faith place as a safe place for someone to call for information about where to get help. A woman or a man who is caught in an abusive scenario might jump at the chance to join in an ongoing break-the-silence initiative from the church. Someone formerly active in a congregation might even say, "I've been wanting to become involved again; when's the first meeting?"

Duration

For what period of time should the group meet? This would depend on the character of the group and the individual needs of its members. An eight week session, perhaps with a break half way through, might be a good format.

Should a person be allowed to come on board half-way through? This is not normally a problem, but since a considerable level of trust would be essential for this particular subject, it might be wise if new members not be encouraged to join after the second or third week. Ways to deal with this would be to arrange another session for the near future and/or to keep offering new opportunities for discussion as interest dictates.

Would a one session "special" forum — after church or mid-week — be helpful? So much would depend on how well the forum was planned, how knowledgeable and credible the resource presenters were, etc. Given the potentially traumatic nature of the subject, standby resources should certainly be available. It could be announced that "Susan X would be happy to talk with anyone after the meeting, or call her at..." Susan X could be a staff member from a women's shelter, or a credible and known counsellor who deals with abuse issues.

Should a formerly abusive male on the mend be announced as a standby resource as well? No. The best intentioned (and changed) male in a position of even informal authority could be a heavy block for a woman starting the healing journey.

Worship

The most significant unique contribution that a congregation could make in the network of support for abuse victims is in the area of worship. Having some kind of informal worship experience in the group sessions would undergird this commitment. A story about the harmful potential of worship will illustrate its power.

At a weekend conference for survivors of child sexual assault, worshippers were invited to say The Lord's Prayer as a brief end-of-the-day worship time. Part-way through the prayer I could hear whimpering. By the time the prayer had concluded, Jenny, one of the conference facilitators (herself a survivor of incest) was already seated on the floor gently rocking Margaret. Her whimpering had by now turned into deep sobbing. Jenny rocked her back and forth in her arms. The sobbing subsided and Margaret drifted into a light sleep.

We spoke of the experience over coffee later, and I discovered for the first time ever that to say "Our Father..." can send shock waves through the heart of an incest survivor. This does not mean that The Lord's Prayer is therefore always off limits in conversation with those who have experienced incest. What it does mean is that prayer and scripture texts have to be used with great sensitivity and care, with respect for the deep feelings of worshippers. Since that experience I have been profoundly aware of the need to take great care in preparing public prayer.

Some form of worship could be part of each discussion group meeting. This could be a short time of uttered — or silent — prayer. To engage with God in prayer or hymn is unquestionably to tap into the very deepest core of hurt places. Even an abuse victim's expressed feeling of abandonment by God is prayer to a God still believed to exist.

The beloved and powerful "Footprints" poem could also be used in a similar context. Perhaps the most common feeling of those who have been hurt by someone they thought they could trust is that of abandonment. The emotional "walking away" by the hurting one is compounded by the belief that friends and family don't care. This is not likely true; they usually don't even know.

SUGGESTIONS FOR CREATIVE DISCUSSION

It would be best if everyone read the whole book as early as possible — to have the broad (and hopeful) picture in mind from the beginning. Male-bashing for its own sake or as part of a wider agenda would be unproductive. If the series were perceived or experienced as such, little of any value would emerge. Yes, the very title of the book is accusatory, and the title of Chapter 1 is provocative. But to identify patriarchy as the fundamental factor in wife abuse is not to accuse all men of being incorrigibly patriarchal. Any man who attends a discussion series on woman abuse would already be signaling a willingness to look reality in the eye and be open to the kind of hard thinking that is needed to help end it. All of us, both men and women, need healing, not blaming.

Starting with an ice-breaker

Since this discussion series will have many emotionally charged moments, an ice-breaking introduction is vital. Knowing something about the others in the group is basic to trust— and a high level of trust will certainly be needed. That "something" need not be earth-shaking, but a safe, even trivial, disclosure helps people learn to talk openly with each other.

There are many effective ice-breakers, but my favorite is called "The Name Game." It is fun, non-threatening, and provides a chance to say something personal safely. Participants are invited (as they wish, not "your turn" around the circle) to comment on their name. It might be the name they use, a nickname, another given name they do not use, or even the name they wish they had. Such sharing usually brings good-hearted hilarity, which is what an ice-breaker is all about.

Jesus, by the way, is from the Hebrew word *yasha'*, which means "to save." The names Isaiah, Joshua and Hosea are from the same word.

Freewheeling or parameters?

There should be freedom to say anything, but it is often important to have parameters. Each of the sessions will assume its own identity. A tight "controlling" format would not be helpful or appreciated, however, given the heavy role of "control" in wife abuse. A good deal of justifiable anger and pain will surface as the trust level of participants deepens. It is therefore even more important to decide whether it should be totally freewheeling or constrained by time limitations on participants. My own inclination is to have no such constraints, and to let the facilitator or the group dynamic itself decide if and when there should be any intervention.

Films

Carefully selected clips from films are a proven motivator to in-depth discussion, but unless a clip is placed within a positive and hopeful context it can be damaging. A vivid portrayal of abuse might have a backfire effect and could itself be abusive.

For example, *The Prince of Tides*, quoted in Chapter 4, includes shocking scenes of wife battering being witnessed by the children. In one scene, the oldest son takes out a rifle and shoots out the living-room TV screen to make his father stop battering his mother during a children's birthday party. When adult men and women describe to me horrible memories of seeing their mother being battered they often seem to relive the experience. One woman actually became childlike in voice and gesture as she spoke to me about her experience. If she were in a discussion group where scenes from *The Prince of Tides* were shown indiscriminately she would be no doubt become extremely agitated, perhaps even emotionally damaged.

This is not to say that groups should avoid portrayals of reality. Neither can the cathartic element of such tools be ignored. Therapeutically it is true that a person who has been violated will experience restoration of mind and spirit by going through, and not around, the pain.

Any film resource selected should enhance discussion and provide insight, not cause more pain. One way in which to get a handle on the appropriateness of a given resource would be to do a "reality check" at regular intervals in order to determine the comfort level of individuals in the group. For example, the week before, a facilitator could ask about using a clip from a film such as *Sleeping With the Enemy*, on stalking, or *The Joy Luck Club*, on a variety of forms of abuse at home.

The timing of the clip in the discussion is crucial. One should avoid the impression of lecturing, or setting out the basic issues or insights for the group. Insights will arise from the group if members feel that their ideas are worth taking seriously. It is one thing to watch the clip of a child witnessing abuse to show the group what this concept means, and quite another to reinforce memories of seeing abuse which have already come from the group. To show the clip too early might block the sharing of personal insights ("compared to that, my experience was trivial"); to show it after some discussion could strengthen an insight already shared.

You may even want to assemble a number of videos for the church library since they are relatively inexpensive now. Someone who might be intimidated by being part of a group might take advantage of a chance to think about abuse issues in private.

Music

It came as a surprise to me to learn that one of the best known Beatles songs contains a reference to woman abuse. "Getting Better" includes these words: "I used to be cruel to my woman; I beat her and kept her apart from the things that she loved."

"Every Breath you Take" by The Police, discussed in Chapter 2, is an undisguised, emotionally abusive, stalking song: "O can't you see, you belong to me... I'll be watching you."

These songs and others are listed as listening resources in Appendix II, and are only a few of the many that could be found in contemporary music. Such a search would make an interesting expedition for you and your group. The cassettes I have listed are only a small representative sample from a host of resources you could dig up with a minimum of effort. Ask anyone who listens to Rock music about abuse scenarios in lyrics and music videos — you'll get an ear full!

Some tapes would make a useful addition to your church library. Linda Allen's *Mama Wanted Me To Be a Rainbow Dancer* and Tom Paxton's *The Paxton Report* contain songs which are especially moving and appropriate for fostering group discussion. In "She Sits on the Table," folk-singer Paxton sings, "The doctor... speaks disapprovingly, 'What did you do to deserve such a beating from him?'" In "The Way of Men" Linda Allen sings, "He beat me bad the day we wed, just thought the beer went to his head." The full lyrics of both these songs are included after these study suggestions.

You may ask, "What is the purpose in having music resources available?" The main reason is that it identifies an abusive scenario "out there" — sung by that folk singer. The arm's length dimension to such an example might free up someone otherwise reticent to be able to say, "My doctor said something like that to me..." Or a doctor in the group might say, "I recall having such attitudes; now I wear a wife-assault-prevention button." (See "Some men are like that" in Chapter 2 and the article "Wearing a wife-assault-prevention button" by Dr. David Gordon White, mentioned in Chapter 7.)

Above all, whatever resources you use should serve the interests of the group and the subject at hand. It would be a misuse of a resource to make it the main theme, letting the rest of the programme fall into place around it. Don't let the tail wag the dog.

These programme sketches have hopefully stimulated your own imagination to think about the best ways that this book could be used by your group. The Bible centres on the family, and the church has traditionally given high priority to family values. The challenge now is to give family *hurting* the urgent attention it deserves. One way to highlight that emphasis in your congregation is to listen to the hard stories about family life told in your own community. They deserve to be heard and honoured. Group discussion can do wonders as we seek ways to stop the hurting and be part of the mending community.

THE WAY OF MEN

by Linda Allen

Well, its hard times most every where,
I think I've had more than my share.
That man of mine's so hard to please,
he's drivin' me right to my knees.

We married young, I was a child,
guess he grew up some kind o' wild.
His daddy beat him 'till he was cloned,
it's the only life he's ever known.

The way of men, it's a hard one, friends;
the hearts of women, so hard to mend.

He beat me bad the day we wed,
just thought the beer went to his head.
He cried he loved me so gently then,
my mama told me it's the way of men.

But then my baby inside me lay,
and he got mad at me one day.
He swung his fists, the sheets turned red,
and later that night she was born dead.

The way of men, it's a hard one, friends;
the hearts of women, so hard to mend.

It isn't love that keeps me here,
somehow he'd find me anywhere.
He said he'd kill me if I'd go away;
may the devil in hell take him today.

If I had wings like a turtle dove,
I'd fly away from the man I loved.
I'd fly so high, I'd fly so free,
that the way of men would not touch me.

The way of men, it's a hard one, friends;
the hearts of women, so hard to mend.

Available from:
Rainbow Dancer Productions
P.O. Box 5881
Bellingham WA 98227
(206) 734-7979

SHE SITS ON THE TABLE

by Tom Paxton

She sits on the table in a dress made of paper,
diplomas all over the wall.
One university, one school of medicine,
she's overwhelmed by it all.

The nurse is all sympathy, voice of experience,
"Let's have a look at that eye.
It's going to look bad for a week, maybe more,
Go on darling, its all right to cry."

"How can I leave him?," she is crying,
"What would I do, where would I go?
He didn't mean it, he will change some day,
O God, how he used to love me so."

The doctor is busy, his manner professional,
she finds she must look at the floor.
He looks at her eye, at her ribs and her arm,
and it seems every last inch is sore.

The doctor is handsome, he smells of cologne,
and his figure's athletically slim.
He speaks disapprovingly, "What did you do
to deserve such a beating from him?"

"How can I leave him?," she is crying,
"What would I do, where would I go?
He didn't mean it, he will change some day,
O God, how he used to love me so."

The policeman is waiting outside in the corridor,
he speaks to her as to a child.
He's friends with her husband, he's angry with her,
and he asks if there'll be charges filed.

She says she's not sure, she needs time to be calmer,
She feels beaten down in disgrace.
The policeman asks isn't she secretly glad
for a man who'll keep her in her place.

"How can I leave him?," she is crying,
"What would I do, where would I go?
He didn't mean it, he will change some day,
O God, how he used to love me so."

Appendix II

Suggestions for Reading, Listening, and Viewing

Also by the Author

Radical Kenosis, Presented to the Department of Philosophy in fulfillment of the degree of Doctor of Philosophy, University of Toronto: 1970. [Unpublished]

"Who Cares for the Victim?," *Crime Victims Newsletter*, Vol. 1, No. 5 (April 1985): 5.

"Blood-Cries: Lament, Wrath, and the Mercy of God," *Touchstone*, Vol. 5, No. 2 (May 1987): 14-25.

"Wounded by Crime," *The United Church Observer*, New Series, Vol. 50, No. 11 (May 1987): 34f.

Toward a Justice That Heals (Toronto: The United Church Publishing House, 1988). (Under the name MacCallum-Paterson.)

"Where Truth Can Be Told, Safely," *Vis-a-Vis*, The Canadian Council on Social Development, Ottawa, Vol. 9, No. 3 (Autumn 1991): 6.

The Face in the Mirror: Five Sermons on Self-Image from the Book of Romans, privately published, 1992, available from The Hamilton Presbytery Resource Centre, St. Giles United Church, 85 Holton Ave. S., Hamilton ON L8M 2L4.

Dr. Jesus: A Wholeness Therapy for Our Day, privately published, 1993, available from The Hamilton Presbytery Resource Centre, St. Giles United Church, 85 Holton Ave. S., Hamilton ON L8M 2L4.

Books

Adams, Carol J., *Woman-Battering* (Minneapolis: Fortress Press, 1994).

Belenky, Mary Field, et al., *Women's Ways of Knowing* (New York: Basic Books, 1986).

Bussert, Joy M.K., *Battered Women: From a Thology of Suffering to an Ethic of Empowerment* (New York: Division of Mission in North America, Lutheran Church in America, 1986).

Brown, Joanne Carlson, and Carole R. Bohn, *Christianity, Partriarchy, and Abuse* (New York: The Pilgrim Press, 1989).

Clarke, R.-L., *Pastoral Care of Battered Women* (Philadelphia: The Westminster Press, 1986).

Conroy, Pat, *The Prince of Tides* (New York: Houghton Mifflin, 1988).

Dekeserdy, Walter, *Woman Abuse in Dating Relationships* (Toronto: Canadian Scholars Press, 1988).

Doehring, Carrie, *No Greater Desecration: Traumatization and Representations of God* (Lanham, Maryland: University Press of America, 1993).

Dyke, Doris Jean, *Crucified Woman* (Toronto: The United Church Publishing House, 1991).

Estes, Clarissa Pinkola, *Women Who Run with the Wolves* (New York: Ballantine Books, 1992).

Fortune, Marie, *Is Nothing Sacred?* (San Francisco: Harper, 1991).

——————, *Keeping the Faith: Questions and Answers for Abused Women* (New York: Harper & Row, 1987).

——————, *Sexual Violence: The Unmentionable Sin* (New York: The Pilgrim Press, 1983).

Forward, Susan, *Toxic Parents* (New York: Bantam Books, 1989).

——————, and Joan Torres, *Men Who Hate Women and the Women who Love Them* (New York: Bantam, 1986).

French, Marilyn, *War Against Women* (New York: Summit Books, 1992).

Gondolf, Edward W., *Man Against Woman: What Every Woman Should Know about Violent Men* (Blue Ridge Summit, Penn.: Tab Books/McGraw-Hill, 1989).

——————, *Man-to-man on Wife Abuse: A Guide for Abusive Men* (Sarasota, Florida: Human Services Press, 1987).

Hennekens, Candace, *Healing Your Life: Recovery from Domestic Abuse* (Fall Creek, Wisconsin: ProWriting Services and Press, 1991).

Hirsh, Miriam F., *Women and Violence* (New York: Van Nostrand Reinhold, 1981).

Hoff, Lee Ann, *Battered Woman as Survivors* (New York: Routledge, 1990).

Horley, Sandra, *The Charm Syndrome: Why Charming Men Can Make Dangerous Lovers* (London: Papermac, 1991).

Horton, Anne L., and Judith A. Williamson, eds., *Abuse and Religion: When Praying Isn't Enough* (Lexington, Mass.: D.C. Heath and Company, 1988).

Hudson, Liam, and Bernardine Jacot, *The Way Men Think* (New Haven: Yale University Press, 1991).

Keen, Sam, *Fire in the Belly: On Being a Man* (New York: Bantam Books, 1991).

Kurland, Morton L., *Coping With Family Violence* (New York: Rosen Publishing Group, 1986).

Leehan, James, *Pastoral Care for Survivors of Family Abuse* (Louisville, Kentucky: Westminster/John Knox Press, 1989).

Lent, Barbara, et al., *Wife Assault: A Medical Perspective* (Toronto: Ontario Medical Association Committee on Wife Assault, 1991).

Lerner, Harriet Goldhor, *The Dance of Anger* (New York: Harper and Row, 1985).

———, *The Dance of Deception* (New York: HarperCollins Publishers, 1993).

Levy, Barnie, ed., *Dating Violence* (New York: Doubleday, 1991).

Lundgren, Eva, *I Herrens Vold* (Oslo, Norway: J.W. Cappelens Forlag, 1985). (English translation — *In the Grip of the Lord* — forthcoming)

———, "The Hand that Strikes and Comforts," *Rethinking Change: Current Swedish Feminist Research* (Uppsala, Sweden: Ord and Form, 1992): 131-58.

MacLeod, Linda, *Battered but Not Beaten... Preventing Wife Battering in Canada* (Ottawa: Canadian Advisory Council on the Status of Women, 1987).

———, *Wife Battering in Canada* (Ottawa: Canadian Advisory Council on the Status of Women, 1980).

Marshall, Pat Freeman, and Marthe Asselin Vaillancourt, *Changing the Landscape: Ending Violence — Achieving Equality, Final Report of The Canadian Panel on Violence Against Women* (Ottawa: Minister of Supply and Services Canada, 1993).

Martin, J.P., ed., *Violence and the Family* (New York: John Wiley and Sons, 1978).

McDill, S. Rutherford, and Linda McDill, *Shattered and Broken* (Tarrytown, N.Y.: Fleming H. Revell Company, 1991).

Nicarthy, Ginny, *The Ones Who Got Away: Women Who Left Abusive Husbands* (New York: Doubleday, 1987).

Norwood, Robin, *Women Who Love Too Much: When You Keep Wishing and Hoping He'll Change* (New York: Simon and Schuster, 1985).

Pagels, Elaine, *Adam, Eve, and the Serpent* (New York: Random House, 1988).

Phillips, Roderick, *Untying the Knot* (Cambridge: Cambridge University Press, 1991).

Roy, Maria, ed., *The Abusive Partner: Analysis of Domestic Battering* (New York: Van Nostrand, 1982).

————, *Children in the Crossfire* (Deerfield Beach, Florida: Health Communications, 1988).

Russell, Diana, *Rape in Marriage* (New York: Macmillan, 1982).

Shupe, Anson D., *Violent Men, Violent Couples: The Dynamics of Domestic Violence* (Lexington, Mass.: Lexington Books, 1987).

Sigler, Robert T., *Domestic Violence in Context: An Assessment of Community Attitudes* (Lexington, Mass.: Lexington Books, 1989).

Soelle, Dorothee, *Suffering* (Philadelphia: Fortress Press, 1975).

Stanton, Elizabeth Cady, *The Woman's Bible* (Seattle, Washington: The Coalition Task Force on Women and Religion, 1974) ISBN 0-9603042-1-5. Originally published in 1898 by the European Publishing Company, New York.

Straus, M., R. Gelles, and S. Steinmetz, *Behind Closed Doors: Violence in the American Family* (Garden City, New Jersey: Anchor/Doubleday, 1980).

Tannen, Deborah, *You Just Don't Understand: Men and Women in Conversation* (New York: Ballantine Books, 1990).

Walker, Lenore, *Terrifying Love: Why Battered Women Kill and How Society Responds* (New York: Harper and Row, 1989).

————, *The Battered Woman Syndrome* (New York: Springer, 1984).

————, *The Battered Woman* (New York: Harper and Row, 1979).

Warshaw, Robin, *I Never Called it Rape: The Ms. Report on Recognizing, Fighting, and Surviving Date and Acquaintance Rape* (New York: Harper and Row, 1988).

Wilson, Lois, *Telling Her Story* (Toronto: The United Church Publishing House, 1992).

Journals

Adams, Carol J., "Help for the Battered," *The Christian Century*, June 29-July 6, 1994: 628-29.

Beaumont, Heather, "Promise Not to Tell," *Homemaker's Magazine*, (October, 1989): 146-53.

Bohn, Diane K., "Domestic Violence and Pregnancy: Implications for Practice," *Journal of Nurse-Midwifery*, Vol. 35, No. 2 (March/April 1990): 86-98.

Bowker, L.H., "Battered Women and the Clergy: An Evaluation," *Journal of Pastoral Care*, Vol. 36, No. 4 (1982): 226-34.

Bulloch, Linda F., and Judith McFarlane, "The Birth-Weight/Battering Connection," *American Journal of Nursing*, Vol. 89, No. 9 (September 1989): 1153-55.

Fortune, Marie, "Picking Up the Broken Pieces: Responding to Domestic Violence," *Church & Society*, Vol. 85, No. 3 (January/February, 1995): 36-47.

Green, Marjorie Ludlow, "Dawn of Terror," *Homemaker's Magazine*, Vol. 27, No. 4 (May, 1992): 14-16+. (A pungent account of terror by Francine Nicholas, an Ontario woman whose husband tried to murder her in front of their six children.)

Helton, Anne, "Battering During Pregnancy," *American Journal of Nursing*, Vol. 86, No. 8 (August 1986): 910-13.

Hurley, D.J., and P. Jaffe, "Children's Observations of Violence: II. Clinical Implications for Children's Mental Health Professionals," *Canadian Journal of Psychiatry*, Vol. 35, No. 6 (August 1990): 471-76 (See Jaffe below.)

Jaffe, G. Peter, Dermot J. Hurley, and David Wolfe, "Children's Observations of Violence: I. Critical Issues in Child Development and Intervention Planning," *Canadian Journal of Psychiatry*, Vol. 35, No. 6 (August 1990): 466-70. (See Hurley above.)

Labatt, Mary, "Violence Against Women," *The Newsletter of the Federation of Women's Teachers Association of Ontario*, Montreal Massacre Memorial Issue, Toronto, Vol. 9, No. 3. (December 1990/January 1991): 2-9.

Parker, Barbara, and Judith McFarlane, "Identifying and Helping Battered Pregnant Women," *American Journal of Maternal Child Nursing*, Vol. 16, No. 3 (May/June 1991): 161-64. An excellent resource list is included in the article.

Randall, Melanie, and Lori Haskell, "Sexual Violence in Women's Lives: Findings from the Women's Safety Project, a Community-Based Survey," *Violence Against Women* (Newbury Park, California: Sage Publications), Vol. 1, No. 1 (March 1995): 6-31.

Rodgers, Karen, "Wife Assault: The Findings of a National Survey," *Juristat*, Canadian Centre for Justice Statistics/Statistics Canada, Vol. 14, No. 9 (March 1994), Catalogue 85-002. (To order, call Marketing Division, Publication Sales, Statistics Canada 1-800-267-6677.)

Sammons, Lucy Newmark, "Battered and Pregnant," *American Journal of Maternal Child Nursing*, Vol. 6, No. 4 (July/August 1981): 246-50.

————, Judith McFarlane, and Elizabeth T. Anderson, "Battered and

Pregnant: A Prevalence Study," *American Journal of Public Health*, Vol. 77, No. 10 (October 1987): 1337-39.

Stirling, Donna, "When an Abuse Victim Murders Her Husband, a Church Steps in to Help," *Jubilee: News of Prison Fellowship Canada* (Oakville, Ontario), Vol. 6, No. 32 (August 1989): 1, 5.

————, "Coming Out of the Closet," *Jubilee: News of Prison Fellowship Canada* (Oakville, Ontario), Vol. 8, No. 36 (September 1990): 1, 7.

Storrie, K., "New Yeast in the Dough: Jesus Transforms Authority," *Daughters of Sarah*, Vol. 10, No. 1 (1984): 10.

Thistlethwaite, S., "Battered Women and the Bible: From Subjection to Liberation," *Christianity and Crisis*, November 16, 1981: 311.

Whipple, Vicky, "Counselling Battered Women From Fundamentalist Churches," *Journal of Marital and Family Therapy*, Vol. 13, No. 3 (July 1987): 251-58.

White, David Gordon, "Wearing a Wife-Assault-Prevention Button: Impact on a Family Practice," *Canadian Medical Association Journal*, Vol. 145, No. 8 (October 15, 1991): 1005-12.

Wilson, Margo, and Martin Daly, "Spousal Homicide," *Juristat*, Canadian Centre for Justice Statistics/Statistics Canada, Vol. 14, No. 8 (March 1994), Catalogue 85-002. (To order, call Marketing Division, Publication Sales, Statistics Canada 1-800-267-6677.)

Young, Anne, and Judith McFarlane, "Preventing Abuse During Pregnancy," *Journal of Nursing Education*, Vol. 30, No. 5 (May 1991): 202-6.

Music

Allen, Linda, "The Way of Men," *Mama Wanted Me To Be a Rainbow Dancer* (Bellingham, Wash.: Nexus Records, 1982). Available from Rainbow Dancer Productions, P.O. Box 5881, Bellingham WA 98227, (206) 734-7979.

Beatles, The, "Getting Better," *Sgt. Pepper's Lonely Hearts Club Band* (Capitol Records/EMI, 1967).

Boston, "To Be a Man," by Tom Scholz, on *Third Stage*, (Los Angeles: MCA Records, 1986).

Chapman, Tracy, "Behind the Wall," *Tracy Chapman* (Elektra Entertainment/Warner Communications Inc., 1988).

Paxton, Tom, "She Sits on the Table," *The Paxton Report* (Mountain Railroad Records, 1980). [MR-52796]

Police, The, "Can't Stand Losing You," *The Police: Greatest Hits* (London: A&M Records, 1992).

————, "Every Breath You Take," *The Police: Greatest Hits* (London: A&M Records, 1992).

Films

Killing Us Softly: Advertising's Image of Women (Cambridge Document, 1980); *And Still Killing Us Softly* (Cambridge Document, 1987) by Jean Kilboure. Both films look at the media's role in perpetuating negative images of women, with its consequent stereotyping and encouraging of male abusive behaviour. Available from Kinetic Films Inc., 408 Dundas Street East, Toronto ON M5A 2A5.

The Crown Prince (National Film Board of Canada, 1988). A drama looking at wife assault from the perspective of children, with insights on how the cycle of violence can be broken.

The Joy Luck Club (Oliver Stone Productions, 1993). This moving multi-generational film tells the stories of women who experienced severe emotional, physical, and sexual abuse from husbands. In one scene a small child witnesses her father's cruelty and is emotionally scarred for life.

The Prince of Tides (Columbia, 1992). An academy award winning movie starring (and directed by) Barbara Streisand and Nick Nolte. The impact of family violence on children is vividly and chillingly portrayed, as well as the positive effect of patient and caring therapeutic counsel.

Seen... But Not Heard (B.C./Yukon Society of Transition Houses, 1993). A docudrama which explores the emotional and physical effects of family violence on the children who witness it. *What About Us?* (B.C./Yukon Society of Transition Houses, 1993). A companion to *Seen, But Not Heard* designed as a counselling tool to help children talk about and cope with their own experiences of abuse. Both by Friday Street Productions and available from Kinetic Films Inc., 408 Dundas Street East, Toronto ON M5A 2A5.

Sleeping With the Enemy (Twentieth Century Fox, 1991). Julia Roberts portrays a woman whose husband tries to control every aspect of her life using emotional, physical, and sexual abuse. When she flees her dread home-prison, he stalks her until he finds her.

Sources

The Anglican Church of Canada
600 Jarvis Street
Toronto ON M4Y 2J6
(416) 924-9192

Violence Against Women: The Report of the General Synod of the Anglican Church of Canada, 1986, 64 pages, is available from any Anglican Book Centre.

Canadian Council on Social Development
441 MacLaren St., 4th floor
Ottawa ON K2P 2H3
(613) 236-8977

The Canadian Council on Social Development produces many publications related to family violence, including *Initiative*, a self-help newsletter, *Vis-a-Vis*, a national newsletter on family violence, and *Perception*, a magazine that encourages dialogue and debate on regional, national, and global issues, as well as personal accounts of experience.

- Rice-Lampert, David, "Multicultural Programs for Men Who Batter," *Vis-a-Vis*, Vol. 12, No. 1 (Summer 1994): 5
- Dosanjh, Raminder, "Indo-Canadian Women Working to End Violence Against Women," *Vis-a-Vis*, Vol. 12, No. 1 (Summer 1994): 6
- Freeman, Janet, "Support Groups for Abused Women," *Vis-a-Vis*, Vol. 11, No. 3 (Winter 1994): 1, 4.
- Price, Lisa, "A Violent Legacy: Exploring the Links Between Child Sexual Abuse and Wife Assault," *Vis-a-Vis*, Vol. 9, No. 2 (Summer 1991): 1, 4.
- Kincaid, Pat J., "The Omitted Reality: Teaching Children Who Witness Family Violence," *Vis-a-Vis*, Vol. 5, No. 2 (Spring/Summer 1987): 1-2.
- Johnson, Holly, and Karen Rodgers, "Canada's survey on violence against women," *Perception*, Vol. 18, No. 1 (June 1994): 3-6.
- "Voices of Aboriginal Women: Aboriginal Women Speak Out About Violence," co-produced with the Native Women's Association of Canada, (1991), 28 pages.

Church Council on Justice and Corrections (CCJC)
507 Bank Street
Ottawa ON K2P 1Z5
(613) 563-1688

The Church Council of Justice and Corrections is involved in many family violence issues, including the "Fire in the Rose" project, dealing with violation, healing, and "living real" in relationship, which utilizes the experiences of a number of congregations across the country. They produce the *Fire in the Rose Newsletter*. See issues I and II, June and November, 1993. Also available, "Family Violence in a Patriarchal Culture," a resource kit, including cassette, co-produced with The Canadian Council on Social Development, 1988.

Health Canada
Family Violence Prevention Division
Communications Division
1st floor, Finance Building
Tunney's Pasture
Ottawa ON K1A 1B5
(613) 957-2938
1-800-267-1291

Health Canada produces an important publication called *Canada's Treatment Programs for Men Who Abuse Their Partners* (1994, ISBN 0-662-22135-4). The National Clearinghouse on Family Violence is part of Health Canada and can provide many relevant publications such as Derek Jehu and Marjorie Gazan, "Psycho-social Adjustment of Women Who Were Sexually Victimized in Childhood or Adolescence," — first published in *Canadian Journal of Community Mental Health*, Vol. 2, No. 2 (September 1983).

A recent project is the Interdisciplinary Project on Domestic Violence, known as "The Mountain and Beyond," with representation from the Canadian Association of Chiefs of Police, Canadian Association of Social Workers, Canadian Medical Association, Canadian Nurses Association, Canadian Psychological Association, Canadian Teachers' Federation, Canadian Bar Association, and the Canadian Council of Churches. *How Do We Get There From Here?* is a resource and planning workbook produced by the project in 1993.

Men Walking Against Male Violence
Box 235, 253 College Street
Toronto ON M5T 1R5
(416) 536-0051

Men Walking Against Male Violence recognizes that "violence against women is much more pervasive and deadly than our society wants to admit." It further believes that "men have to begin to take responsibility as individuals, and in relationship with other men, to end our violence against women and children."

Mothers On Trial
707 Dundas St. W.
Toronto ON M5T 2W6
(416) 761-7734

Mothers on Trial is an unincorporated and voluntary group of women who have experienced or are still experiencing the crisis of involvement in the family law system. They draw attention to abusive proceedures and practices that they perceive as experienced in the courts by women who have left a violent marriage. See their publication *Family Violence = Family Law Violence: Women's Experiences in Family Law Proceedings*, published with the cooperation of the Ontario Women's Directorate and the United Way of Greater Toronto, August, 1993.

Ontario Women's Directorate
2 Carlton St., 12th floor
Toronto ON M5B 2M9
(416) 314-0300

The Women's Directorate sponsors the "Wife Assault: It's a Crime" campaign. Posters, buttons and a 6-page brochure are available. The Directorate also produces a newsletter, "Education Wife Assault."

Statistics Canada
1-800-267-6677

Statistics Canada provides publications on all aspects of Canadian life including justice. Some publications are free and others are available at cost.

The United Church of Canada
3250 Bloor St. W., Ste. 300
Etobicoke ON M8X 2Y4
(416) 231-5931
fax (416) 231-3103

The Division of Mission in Canada includes a Family Education and Justice section. One of their publications is "Women Who Live in Abusive Relationships," 7 pages, ISBN 0-88622-237. Also available is *Ending Violence in Families: A Training Program for Pastoral Care Workers*, by Roberta Morris, 1988.

The Church also publishes several periodicals including *Exchange*, *Women's Concerns*, *Mandate*, and *The United Church Observer*, which frequently deal with family issues.

- Devine, Nancy, "Fire in the Rose," *Mandate*, Vol. 24, No. 6 (November 1993): 9-11.

- *Mandate*, Special Edition on the Ecumenical Decade of Churches in Solidarity with Women, Vol. 22, No. 3, (1991).
- Mitchell, Karen, "You, Violence, and Your Church," *Exchange*, (Winter 1985): 23-25
- Perkins, Dale, "Men Against Violence Against Women," *Exchange*, (Winter 1985): 40
- FairHeart, Joanna, "The Bible and Violence Against Women," *Women's Concerns*, Issue 33 (Fall 1986): 5-6.

White Ribbon Campaign
(Men Working to End Men's Violence Against Women)
220 Yonge St.
Galleria Offices, Ste. 104
Toronto ON M5B 2H1
1-800-328-2228
(416) 596-1513
fax (416) 596-8359

The White Ribbon Campaign is a Canadian men's initiative started in 1991 to work against men's violence towards women. In 1993 they sponsored a campaign of concern about violent video games, especially a Sega game called "Night Trap." In 1994 they expanded that campaign, working with Boards of Education, into the "No Joy in Violent Toys" campaign, designed as part of a broader effort to raise awareness about the impact of violent toys on legitimizing violence as a way of dealing with frustration, anger, and conflict.

The White Ribbon Campaign also provides education kits for students, such as "Building Healthy Relationships" on dating behaviour, due to be released for Valentine's Day, 1995. The group also produces a popular publication called "What Every Man Can Do To Help End Men's Violence Against Women." The White Ribbon Campaign does not, on principle, accept government funding, in the belief that public money should be spent on women's projects and shelters.

Appendix III

The Violence Against Women Survey

On November 18th, 1993, Statistics Canada released the results of a national survey (excluding the Yukon and the Northwest Territories) on male violence toward women that had been conducted on behalf of Health Canada. Approximately 12,300 women 18 years of age and older were interviewed by telephone in depth about their experiences of physical and sexual violence since the age of 16, and about their perceptions of their personal safety. All the women were, or had been married, or lived in a common-law relationship. The responses were weighted to represent the 10,498,000 women over 18 in the Canadian population. Estimates based on this proportion of all Canadian women, as well as the methodology, are expected to be within 1.2% of the true proportion 19 times out of 20.

Based on experience of previous crime victimization surveys, interviewers were trained to recognize and respond appropriately to cues indicating that the woman might be concerned about being overheard. If a *current* state of abuse was disclosed, or if there was evident distress, telephone numbers of local support services were offered. A toll free telephone number also provided an opportunity to call back and check the legitimacy of the survey, or to continue the interview at a more convenient time and place.

Note: In every case "marital partner" (and the correlative expression "ever been married") may be understood to include common-law relationships. Most of the percentages given below total more than 100% in a given category; this is due to multiple responses to the question by the same woman. C = Current, P = Previous, P'ner = Partner.

1. PHYSICAL AND SEXUAL ASSAULT BY A PARTNER

Twenty-nine percent of Canadian women who have ever been married or living with a man have been assaulted by their partner. Three percent of women were assaulted by their partner in the twelve months prior to the survey.

Lifetime rates of woman assault were significantly higher in cases of previous marriages (48% of women with a previous marriage were assaulted by a previous marital partner) than in cases of current marriages (15% of currently married have been assaulted by their current partner).

A. Rates by province are:

British Columbia	36%
Alberta	34%
Nova Scotia	32%
Manitoba	30%
Ontario	29%
Saskatchewan	28%
New Brunswick	26%
P.E.I.	25%
Quebec	25%
Newfoundland	17%

B. Rates of violence for legal marriages and common-law relationships vary slightly:

- Fifteen percent of currently married women and 18% of women living in a common-law relationship have experienced violence by their current partner.

C. Newer marital partnerships have the highest rates of violence:

- Marriages of two years or less had the highest rates (8%) of violence in the 12 months prior to the survey, while partnerships of more than 20 years were 1%.

D. The rate of woman assault among women 18 to 24 years of age is four times the national average:

Aged	18-24	12%
	25-34	4%
	35-44	3%
	45 and over	1%

E. **In recent years, some research has suggested that women with disabilities are at greater risk of victimization:**

- Thirty-nine percent of ever-married women with a disability or a disabling health problem reported physical or sexual abuse by a partner over the course of their married lives, compared to 29% of the total female population.

F. **Alcohol is a prominent factor in woman assault:**

- In one-half of all violent partnerships the perpetrator was usually drinking.
- The rate of woman assault for women currently living with men who drank regularly (at least four times per week) was triple the rate of women whose partners never drank.
- Women were at six times the risk of violence by partners who frequently consumed five or more drinks at one time, compared to women whose partners never drank.

2. TYPES OF ABUSE

A. Emotional Abuse

	C or P P'ner	*C P'ner*	*P P'ner*
He is jealous and doesn't want her talking to other men	19%	6%	38%
He tries to limit contact with family or friends	16%	4%	33%
He insists on knowing who she is with and where she is at all times	22%	10%	36%
He calls her names to put her down or make her feel bad	21%	7%	39%
He prevents her from knowing about or having access to the family income, even if she asks	10%	2%	22%
Any emotional abuse	35%	17%	59%

B. Physical Abuse

- One-third of women who were assaulted by a partner feared for their lives at some point during the abusive relationship.
- Forty-five percent of wife assault cases resulted in physical injury

to the woman. The most frequent types of injuries reported were bruises (90%), followed by cuts, scratches and burns (33%), broken bones (12%), and fractures (11%).

- Almost 10% of injured women also stated that they suffered internal injuries and miscarriages.

C. Type of Violence

	C or P P'ner	*C P'ner*	*P P'ner*
Total Wife Assault	29%	15%	48%
Threatened to hit her with something	19%	7%	35%
Threw something	11%	4%	21%
Pushed, grabbed or shoved	25%	12%	40%
Slapped	15%	4%	30%
Kicked, bit or hit with fist	11%	2%	22%
Hit her with something	6%	1%	12%
Beat her up	9%	1%	19%
Choked her	7%	1%	14%
Threatened to use gun or knife	5%	1%	10%
Sexual assault	8%	2%	17%

D. Severity of Abuse

- In many cases, the injury was severe enough to require medical attention; approximately four-in-ten women injured by a marital partner saw a doctor or a nurse for medical attention.
- In almost one-third of the cases, the woman had to take time off because of abuse. Of those who were physically injured, 50% had to take time off.
- Weapons were used by 44% of violent spouses: 38% of women had something thrown at them by a current or previous spouse, 19% were hit with something that could hurt them, and 16% had a gun or knife used on them.

E. Frequency of Abuse

- In almost two-thirds of woman assault cases the violence occurred on more than one occasion. Repeated or ongoing abuse was more often reported in relationships that had ended, indicating that many women leave relationships with more frequent or serious violence.

- Three-quarters of women who had experienced violence by a previous partner were subjected to multiple assaults, 41% on more than ten occasions.
- Thirty-nine percent of women currently living with an abusive partner experienced more than one violent episode, 10% with more than one.

F. Psychological Consequences

- Eighty-five percent of women reporting assault indicated that they experienced some type of emotional effect, e.g., anger, fear, becoming more cautious and less trusting, lowered self-esteem, depression, anxiety, feelings of shame and guilt, and having problems relating to men.
- Approximately 25% of the women reporting assault used alcohol, drugs or medication to help them cope with the situation.

G. When abuse started

- Sixteen percent of women abused in a previous or current marriage indicated that the abuse started before marriage (17% for women in a legal marriage, 28% for those living common-law).
- Twenty-one percent of abused women were assaulted during pregnancy; 40% of these women stated that the abuse began during their pregnancy.

H. Women Who Left an Abusive Partner

Forty-three percent of women left temporarily or permanently because of abuse, based on such factors as these:

- Seventy-four percent of those who reported an incident to the police left (18% for those who did not report)
- Fifty-seven percent because they feared for their lives (36% of those who did not fear for their lives)
- Sixty percent of women whose children had witnessed the violence (as against 34% in cases where the violence was not witnessed by children).

Seventy-seven percent of women who left stayed with friends or relatives, 13% moved to a transition house or shelter, 13% into a place of their own, and 5% stayed in a motel.

Almost three-quarters of women who left eventually returned home. Of those who returned home, 31% did so for the sake of their children, 24% in order to give the relationship another chance, 17% because of a partner's promise to change, and 9% because of lack of money or housing.

Eighty-one percent of those whose partner received some form of counselling returned home, but 70% did so even though the partner received no counselling.

I. The Cycle of Violence

Research in this area suggests that witnessing violence against one's *mother* increases the likelihood that a woman will be in an abusive relationship and that a man will be violent toward his spouse.

- Seventeen percent of abused women stated that, to the best of their knowledge, their fathers were violent toward their mothers
- Nine percent of currently married and 17% of previously married women reported violence by their fathers-in-law toward their wives.
- Fifty-five percent of women whose fathers-in-law were violent endured more severe and repeated types of violence than women whose fathers-in-law were not violent. The rate is 35% for those whose partners had not witnessed violence.

J. Impact on Children Who Witness Violence at Home

- Thirty-nine percent of women in violent marriages reported that children had witnessed it.
- In 52% of those situations women had feared for their lives; in 61% women were injured.

K. Police Involvement

In the early 1980's, *mandatory* domestic assault charging policies were initiated across the country (i.e., previously it was optional, and a charge had to be laid by the victim). Charges were laid in about 26% of wife assault cases in this study.

- In 84% of reported cases the police responded by seeing the woman.
- In 28% of cases the perpetrator was arrested and charges were laid.
- Women were twice as likely to lay charges if children had witnessed the violence.
- Women were four times more likely to report to the police if at some point a weapon was used against her.
- Forty-nine percent of women who had been abused more than ten times reported at least once to the police, compared to 6% of those who experienced only one episode.

- Fifty percent of women who contacted the police said that they were satisfied with the way the police handled the case.
- In 20% of cases, the police put the woman in touch with a community service agency.
- Sixty-five percent of women were satisfied with the way they were treated in court.
- In 45% of cases the violence decreased or stopped following police intervention, but in 40% of cases there was no change in men's behaviour after police intervention. In 10% of cases the violence increased.

Reasons for not reporting assault included the following:

Too minor	52%
Wanted to keep incident private	10%
Didn't want or need help	10%
Didn't want to get involved with police or the courts	9%
Fear of partner	8%
Didn't think police could help	7%
Shame/embarrassment	5%
Didn't want him arrested	3%
Other	3%

L. Use of Social Services

Total that used a social service	24%
Contacted a transition home (shelter)	8%
Stayed at a transition home	6%
Crisis centre/line	4%
Women's centre	3%
Community/family centre	5%
Another counsellor	15%
Used none of above services	75%

Though the use of formal social services was fairly low, most women who did take advantage of a social service found it helpful:

Counsellor	83%
Transition home, shelter	81%
Crisis centre	77%
Women's centre	73%
Community/family centre	65%

Women were twice as likely to use a social service if they were injured, or if their children witnessed the violence.

Reasons for not using a social service:

Didn't want/need help	40%
Too minor	25%
Didn't know of any	16%
None available	14%
Shame/embarrassment	6%
Got help elsewhere	5%
Didn't want relationship to end	2%
Keep private	2%
Other	5%

Sources of support:

Family	45%
Friends and neighbours	44%
Doctor	25%
Religious Leader	7%

Twenty-two percent of the women reporting violence had never told anyone about it before the survey and 10% had feared for their lives yet told no one.

For a general background statement and commentary on the report see Holly Johnson and Karen Rodgers, "Canada's survey on violence against women," *Perception*, Vol. 18, No. 1, Canadian Council on Social Development: pp. 3-6. Both authors are senior analysts at the Canadian Centre for Justice Statistics and both worked on the survey.

Adapted from Statistics Canada, *Juristat*, Catalogue 85-002, Vol. 14, No. 9, 21 pages, 1994 ($3.60). Reproduced by authority of the Minister of Industry, 1994.

Readers wishing additional information on data provided through the cooperation of Statistics Canada may obtain copies of related publications by mail from:

Publications Sales, Statistics Canada, Ottawa, Ontario, K1A 0T6, by calling (613) 951-7277 or toll-free 1-800-267-6677. Readers may also facsimile their order by dialing (613) 951-1584.

Appendix IV

Historical Attitudes To Wife Abuse

There is some debate among historians as to the extent of marital violence — most of it inflicted on the wife — in the past. Keith Wrightson, for example, has argued that in seventeenth-century England "wife-battering was certainly known," but that there is no evidence that "physical violence was an accepted feature of lower-class marriages." Edward Shorter, on the other hand, has suggested that "as a practical matter, wife-beating was universal." There are, of course, immense problems of evidence. Wife beating came to the notice of the ecclesiastical and secular courts in divorce, separation, and other kinds of cases, but there is no way of knowing how representative the couples involved were of married couples generally. If wife beating were very common, and especially if it was a socially accepted form of behaviour, it would be unlikely to turn up in court cases, except incidentally (as it does) or, perhaps, when the violence was particularly severe. The absence of systematic records of wife beating, then, might indicate that it was very common or very uncommon. My assessment is that it was common, and that a moderate level of violence within marriage was expected. Moreover, to the extent that it was expected, moderate violence could be accommodated within a workable marital relationship, and was not a sign of marriage breakdown.

There is certainly plenty of evidence for the social acceptability of wife beating. Most Western legal codes allowed husbands to inflict what was termed "moderate correction" on their wives. "Moderate" was not defined precisely, but there were various guidelines. The violence should not draw blood, for example, and if a stick were used, it should be no thicker than a man's thumb. (This is the origin of the term "rule of thumb.") As for "correction," the point was that a husband might not beat his wife at random or on a whim, but only in order to correct or punish her. "Moderate correction," then, should be interpreted as a part of the husband's general ability in law to control his wife. The underlying legal justification was that because a husband could be held legally responsible for his wife's actions, he should have the right to control her actions and to punish her when necessary. Such rights were recognized by canon law and the customary laws of medieval Europe. The thirteen-century customary law of Beauvais (France) went further than most in holding that "it is licit for the man to beat his wife, without bringing about death or disablement, when she refuses her husband anything."

Such precepts were challenged in the sixteen and seventeenth centuries. In England a number of commentators (many of them Puritans) argued that violence was not a legitimate part of a husband's authority. William Ames, for one, wrote that "it is by no means the part of any Husband, to correct his Wife with blowes," while Nathaniel Hardy argued that "surely we may account them besotted in their minds, or possessed with a divel who lay violent hands upon their wives." This shift of attitudes was manifested in a handful of legal codes. In Calvin's Geneva spouse beating was made a crime, and between 1564 and 1569 some sixty-one men and two women were convicted of it and excommunicated. Similarly, in Puritan Massachusetts the first code of law in 1641 emancipated married women from having to tolerate "bodily correction or stripes from her husband, unlesse it be in his owne defence upon her assault." In 1650 the law specified fines of up to ten pounds or a whipping for a husband who struck his wife or a wife her husband.

Limitations on the right of "moderate correction" were sparse, however, and even where they were applied it is not clear how much impact they might have had on deeply entrenched beliefs about the relative power of husband and wife. While it is possible to find popular support for the view that wife beating was wrong, there is more evidence of support for the traditional power of men to control their wives by force if necessary. Against the sixteenth-century German saying that "To strike a woman brings little honour to a man," we can range proverbs such as "Don't expect any good from an ass, a nut or a woman unless you have a stick in your hand" (Languedoc), and "Good or bad, the horse gets the spur. Good or bad, the wife gets the stick" (Provence).

There were challenges to the principle of moderate correction in some eighteenth-century legal codes, such as a 1790 French law that provided heavier penalties for assaults on women than for assaults on men. But it was not until the nineteenth century that legislation and case law began systematically to criminalize wife beating or to give beaten women some kind of redress in law. A series of laws in England in the second half of the nineteenth century enabled the courts to punish wife beaters with imprisonment, fines, and floggings. In 1878 aggravated assault was made a ground for a judicial separation, although it did not become a ground for divorce until 1937. In 1891 the husband's right to moderate correction was abolished.

There was a similar trend in the United States. An 1824 Mississippi judgment limited a husband to only "moderate chastisement in cases of emergency" (it did not define a matrimonial emergency), and the general tendency was to provide penalties for wife beating, despite the concern of some judges about the involvement of the courts in what they considered private matters. Even so, it was far from easy for women to obtain legal redress against their husbands. Judges in revolutionary France often insisted that the proper course of action for beaten married women was divorce, not an action against their husbands for assault. Individual judges elsewhere explicitly or implicitly upheld the traditional power of husbands. In the 1887 Yorkshire (England) assizes, for example, Judge Edward Cox heard the case of a woman who had been knocked down by her husband and then beaten about the head with a poker until the blood flowed. Her offense had been to go to "some amusement" without first getting her husband's permission. Despite the fact that the assault went well beyond the accepted limits of "moderate," and despite recent legislation against wife beating, the judge ruled that the husband's violence was within the bounds of "reasonable chastisement" and stated that it was a "waste of time to bring these cases before the jury." Other judges, however, condemned wife beating as "barbaric," calling the perpetrators "brutes," "tyrants," and "monsters."

The number of wife-beating cases that came before the courts was small, however. If we assume that the phenomenon was widespread, we should explain the rarity of cases in terms of the absence of effective laws, the recognition that laws were applied inconsistently, and the simple domestic reality that a wife's prosecuting her husband would almost certainly worsen, rather than improve, their relationship....

... Bearing in mind that wife beating includes a wide range of behaviour, from a single and relatively mild slap to persistent vicious assaults, the overall image of the phenomenon is complex. There is evidence at all levels of society of support for the traditional husbands' right of correction and of opposition to domestic violence in any form. It remains unclear whether there were class differences in wife beating: Opposition to it was expressed by middle- and upper-class commentators and by working class charivaris. There was a prevailing belief by the middle classes that violence was more characteristic of the lower ("dangerous") classes, but the social pervasiveness of domestic violence in modern Western society should dissuade us from accepting these earlier beliefs uncritically. Nor, in attempting to determine the extent of wife beating, should we rely too heavily on reported cases. The number of reported domestic assaults in London declined in the second half of the nineteenth century, but it is possible that the decline was a result of wife beating's having been driven into the private recesses of the Victorian household, where it was less susceptible to social surveillance. It is possible, too, that increasingly severe penalties — by 1882, magistrates could have wife beaters flogged and exposed in a public pillory — deterred women from reporting violence more than it deterred men from committing it.

Throughout several centuries of discussion and legal changes, wife beating seems to have persisted relentlessly. We may quote or cite the findings of numerous historians to support this point. In colonial New England, wife beating is described as "tacitly condoned." In eighteenth-century Languedoc it is reported that "it is common enough to hear wives express the just fear they have of being chastised and beaten by their husbands. Among those of low and modest condition it seems that such apprehensions were accepted without suggesting abnormal brutality." In late nineteenth-century London wife beating is described as "normal" when it served a disciplinary function. Some industrial districts of England and Scotland were known as "kicking districts" after the incidence of assaults on wives. In Ireland in the early twentieth century childlessness was customarily blamed on the wife and entitled the husband to "bounce a boot off her now and then for it." Obstetrical literature often mentioned in passing that women miscarried after being beaten: "The doctors were not particularly distressed by wife-beating, but mentioned it casually along with other medical details."

Wife beating, in short, seems to have been a constant in Western society, sometimes criticized and perhaps increasingly so with the passage of time, but always pervasive.

To insist on the normalcy of wife beating is not to condone it, but rather to describe the continuous presence of this coarse thread of behaviour in the fabric of married life. Its apparent extent and social universality, however, raises the question whether this form of violence betokened marriage breakdown. We should have to conclude that insofar as violence did not fall outside the expectations of marriage, it was not a sign of breakdown. Given their experience of family life as daughters and witnesses to other marriages, women must have expected to be struck at some time by their husbands. It was, then, only when the degree of frequency of violence was significantly greater than expected that we can think of it as indicating breakdown. Even then we must allow for changes in expectations when considerations of children, financial dependence, or other factors simply gave women no alternative but to tolerate violence. In the final analysis we must accept that marriage breakdown is a matter of individual as of social definition, and that if a couple, in their own personal and social context, were able to integrate a degree of violence into their conceptions of an acceptable and functioning marriage, it would be arrogant of historians to contradict them.

— from Roderick Phillips, *Untying the Knot*, pp. 97-102.

Appendix V
Women's Shelters

Every province has a list of shelters where a woman may seek counsel and accommodation for herself and her children if necessary. Information about women's shelters is confidential and available by referral only in order to protect the safety of residents. Local information or family service agencies would also be helpful in locating the nearest shelter.

Canada
Status of Women Canada
Constitution Square Building
360 Albert Street, Suite 700
Ottawa ON K1A 1C3
(613) 995-7835

British Columbia
British Colombia Ministry
of Women's Equality
756 Fort Street
Victoria BC V8V 1X4
(604) 387-0413

Alberta
Women's Policies and Programs
Women's and Seniors' Secretariat
Peace Hill Tower
1660-10405 Jasper Ave.
Edmonton AB T5J 4R7
(403) 422-4927

Saskatchewan
Saskatchewan Women's
Secretariat
1914 Hamilton Street, 3rd floor
Regina SK S4P 4V4
(306) 787-2329

Manitoba
Manitoba Women's Directorate
100-175 Carlton Street
Winnipeg MB R3C 3H9
(204) 945-3476

Ontario
Ontario Women's Directorate
2 Carlton St., 12th floor
Toronto ON M5B 2M9
(416) 314-0300

Ontario Women's Directorate
107C Johnson Ave.
Thunder Bay ON P7B 2V9
(807) 345-6084

Québec
Associée à la Condition
Feminine
Edifice H, Bureau 2700
875 Grande Allée Est
Québec City PQ G1R 4Y8
(418) 643-9052

New Brunswick

New Brunswick currently has no central agency responsible for referrals. Please contact the transition house nearest you for more information.

Accueil Sainte-Famille
C.P. 3001
Tracadie NB E0C 2B0
(506) 395-2212

Crossroads for Women Inc.
P.O. Box 1247
Moncton NB E1C 8P9
(506) 853-0811

Escale Madavic
C.P. 411
Edmundston NB E3V 3L1
(506) 739-6265

Fundy House Inc.
P.O. Box 234
St. Stephen NB E3L 1G0
(506) 466-4485

Gignoog Transition House
P.O. Box 3385
Fredericton NB E3A 5H2
(506) 458-1224

Hestia House
P.O. Box 7135, Stn. A
Saint John NB E2L 4S5
(506) 634-7570

Maison de "Passage" Home Inc.
C.P. 1284
Bathurst NB E2A 4J1
(506) 546-9540

Maison Notre Dame II
C.P. 578
Campbellton NB E3N 3G9
(506) 753-4703

Miramichi Emergency Centre for Women
King George Highway
P.O. Box 249
Newcastle NB E1V 3M3
(506) 622-8865

Sanctuary House
P.O. Box 1014
Woodstock NB E0J 2B0
(506) 325-9452

Sussex Vale Transition House
P.O. Box 2184
Sussex NB E0E 1P0
(506) 432-6999

Women in Transition House Inc.
P.O. Box 1143
Fredericton NB E3B 5H2
(506) 454-1498

Nova Scotia

Nova Scotia Women's Directorate
P.O. Box 486
5151 Terminal Rd.
Halifax NS B3J 2R7
(902) 424-5820

Prince Edward Island

Transition House Association
(Anderson House)
c/o Voluntary Resource Centre
81 Prince St.
Charlottetown PE C1A 4R3
(902) 368-8658
Emergency (902) 892-0960 (toll free)

Newfoundland
Newfoundland Women's Policy Office
Confederation Building
West Block, 4th floor
P.O. Box 8700
St. John's NF A1B 4J6
(709) 729-5098

Yukon
Yukon Women's Directorate
P.O. Box 2703
2071 2nd Avenue
Whitehorse YT Y1A 2C6
(403) 667-3030

Northwest Territories
Status of Women
P.O. Box 1320
Yellowknife NT X1A 2L9
(403) 920-6177

United States
National Organization for Women (NOW)
1000 - 16th Street Northwest, Suite 700
Washington DC 20036
(202) 331-0066

United States Department of Labor — Boston
Women's Bureau
1 Congress St., 11th floor
Boston MA 02114
(617) 565-1988

United States Department of Labor — Philadelphia
Women's Bureau
Gateway Building, Room 2450
3535 Market Street
Philadelphia PA 19104
(215) 596-1183

United States Department of Labor — Chicago
Women's Bureau
230 South Dearborn Street, Room 1022
Chicago IL 60604
(312) 353-6985

United States Department of Labor — Kansas City
Women's Bureau
1100 Main Street, Suite 1230
Kansas City MI 64105
(816) 426-6108

United States Department of Labor — Dallas
Women's Bureau
525 Griffin Building, Room 731
Dallas TX 75202
(214) 767-6985

United States Department of Labor — San Francisco
Women's Bureau
71 Stevenson Street, Suite 927
San Francisco CA 94105

Appendix VI

Reality, with Hope

Violence Against Women in the Bible
A Darkside Lectionary

The numerous depictions of violence toward women in the Bible are excluded in the three-year cycle Common Lectionary which is in general use in the church. Texts which reflect violent and negative attitudes toward women receive scant attention in biblical studies courses in theological colleges. Clergy and lay persons alike are often astonished when reminded that these stories are *in scripture*, and those who are hurt at home invariably gasp when told that *their* stories are mirrored in the Bible.

These stories need to be read carefully, with empathy. They concern women who were subjected to a wide range of male abuse. It matters not that some are steeped in prehistoric mythology, or reflect attitudes that are no longer tolerated. The fact that they have remained relatively ignored within the canon of scripture indicates a general, though undeclared, acceptance of the basic image of womanhood which underlies them. Those who are hurt by such images are further damaged by the church's silence.

That's the bad news. The good news is that the Bible, as a whole, celebrates the restoration of dignity. To believe oneself to be a daughter or son of God is in itself an affirmation of one's worth. The Cry, Response, and Mending motifs draw out this conviction in such a way that the whole biblical salvation story is about the *recovery* of that which was lost.

The Common Lectionary consists of an Old Testament, Psalm, Epistle, and Gospel reading clustered around a more or less unified theme. Here the Psalm readings are combined with the Old Testament selections. Unlike the Common Lectionary, these readings are not tied to the church year but they are grouped around fifty-two Mending themes. The readings in each cluster reflect either the Cry or the Response motif, but the Mending motif is meant to be stressed in every case.

1.	Ruth 1:6-18; Psalm 2 I Corinthians 11:1-16 John 11:1-6	Serenity at home: a promise I
2.	Leviticus 18:6-18 Romans 12:1-21 Matthew 10:34-39	Serenity at home: a promise II
3.	Gen. 16:1-16; 21:9-21; Ps. 55 I John 4:18f Luke 23:27-31	Flight from danger
4.	Isaiah 54:1-8; 66:7-13 Revelation 12:1-16 Luke 1:8-25, 57f	Safety during pregnancy I
5.	II Kings 8:7-15 I Thessalonians 5:1-11 Luke 1:26-45; 2:1-7	Safety during pregnancy II
6.	Amos 1:13-15; Micah 4:9-13 Galatians 4:21-31 Luke 1:46-56	Safety during pregnancy III
7.	Job 17:1-5; Ps. 137 Ephesians 6:1-7 Luke 9:46-48	Caring for hurting children I
8.	Deut. 1:26-33 I Thess. 2:3-8 Mark 7:24-30	Caring for hurting children II
9.	Daniel 6:21-24 Acts 7:17-22 Matt. 7:7-12	Caring for hurting children III
10.	Gen. 3:1-7; Ruth 2:8-23 Rev. 12:7-17 John 4:7-26	Women honoured I
11.	I Kings 21:1-16 or II Kings 9:21-36 I Cor. 14:33b-40 John 4:27-42	Women honoured II
12.	Gen. 3:8-21 Eph. 5:22-33 Luke 7:36-50	Free from subordination I
13.	Gen. 19:1-11 Colossians 3:18-25 Mark 12:39-44	Free from subordination II
14.	Nehemiah 5:1-13 I Peter 2:18-3:7 Luke 8:1-3	Free from subordination III
15.	Gen. 24:45-67 Titus 2:3-5 Matt. 19:1-10	Free from subordination IV

16.	Esther 1:13-22 Romans 7:1-3 Mark 3:31-35	Free from subordination V
17.	Gen. 6:1-4 I Cor. 14:34-35 Mark 16:9-11	Free from subordination VI
18.	Zechariah 5:5-11 II Timothy 1:3-7 John 2:1-11	Women's self-worth I
19.	Numbers 31:8-20 I Peter 3:1-6 Luke 15:8-10	Women's self-worth II
20.	Gen. 28:1-9; 29:15-20 I Tim. 5:3-16 Luke 2:36-38	Women's self-worth III
21.	Ezekiel 22:6-11, 33:26 Romans 5:9-13 Luke 10:38-41	Women's self-worth IV
22.	Deut. 28:30-32 or Isaiah 65:17-25 Romans 9:20-26 Luke 11:27	Women's self-worth V
23.	Deut. 22:10-14 Romans 10:4-9 Luke 12:42-48	Women's self-worth VI
24.	I Kings 1:1-4 I Cor. 7:1-5 John 15:12-17	Women's self-worth VII
25.	Lev. 12 Hebrews 8 Luke 2:22-38	Women's self-worth VIII
26.	Judges 11:29-40 Romans 16:1-16 Matt. 2:13-23	Women's autonomy I
27.	Gen. 20 I Cor. 7:10-11 Mark 15:33-41	Women's autonomy II
28.	Isa. 3:11-4:1 I Peter 3:7 Matt. 13:33	Women's strength I
29.	Nahum 3:10-13; Jud. 4:4-10 Acts 5:1-11 Luke 18:1-8	Women's strength II
30.	Isa. 19:16; Jer. 50:33-38 Acts 16:11-15 Luke 17:30-37	Women's strength III

31. Esther 1:1-12 Hebrews 11:29-40 John 12:1-8	Women's sexual integrity I
32. Num. 5:11-31; Hosea 1:1-7, 2:1-3 Hebrews 13 John 8:2-11	Women's sexual integrity II
33. Deut. 22:13-27 Romans 1:24-32 Matt. 5:27-30	Women's sexual integrity III
34. II Samuel 13:1-22 I Thess. 4:1-8 Matt. 5:38-42	New dignity after rape I
35. Deut. 22:28ff or Jer. 9:17-20 Gal. 5:16-21 Matt. 5:1-11	New dignity after rape II
36. II Samuel 15:16; 16:21-23; 20:3 I Cor. 5 Matt. 1:18-25	New dignity after rape III
37. Deut. 21:10-17 Eph. 5:1-6 Matt. 10:26-31	New dignity after rape IV
38. I Sam. 30:1-6 Rev. 21:1-8 Matt. 5:43-48	New dignity after rape V
39. Jud. 19:1-10 I Cor. 6:12-20 Matt. 25:31-46	New dignity after rape VI
40. Jud. 19:22-30; Lam. 5:11 I Cor. 7:8-9 John 10:1-10	New dignity after rape VII
41. Gen. 34:1-34 I Cor. 7:32-40 Luke 13:1-5	New dignity after rape VIII
42. Amos 2:6-8 I Peter 3:8-17 Luke 20:27-40	New dignity after rape IX
43. II Kings 5:1-19 James 3:5-12 Luke 13:10-17	Women's initiative in healing I
44. Lev. 15:1-33 James 5:13-16 Luke 8:40-56	Women's initiative in healing II
45. Song of Songs 5:6-8 Acts 2:14-21 Luke 23:50-56; 24:1-10	Women's initiative in healing III

46. Num. 30:3-15 Philippians 2:5-11 Luke 22:24-27	Relinquishing male power
47. Jer. 44:15-30 Rev. 2:12-17 Matt. 7:1-5	The end of woman blaming I
48. Num. 25:1-16 Romans 14:13-23 Matt 11:7-19	The end of woman blaming II
49. Ezra 10:1-44 I Cor. 7:12-16 Luke 4:16-30	The end of woman blaming III
50. Num. 12:1-16 Gal. 5:22-6:10 Matt. 25:1-13	The end of woman blaming IV
51. Lam. 1:4-12; 3:51-66 Rev. 18:1-24 Matt. 11:28-30	Breaking the silence
52. Deut. 25:11-12; Ruth 3 Rev. 2:18-29 Matt. 26:6-13	Misogyny unmasked

Scripture Index

Anecdotal Index

Index